EXAM FIRST AID
Multiple-Choice Exams

EXAM FIRST AID
Multiple-Choice Exams

JENNIFER KAMITA
Clinical Professor of Law
Loyola Law School Los Angeles

CHRISTOPHER HAWTHORNE
Clinical Professor of Law
Loyola Law School Los Angeles

SASCHA BENSINGER
Former Clinical Professor of Law
Loyola Law School Los Angeles

Published by Wolters Kluwer in New York.

Wolters Kluwer Legal & Regulatory US serves customers worldwide with CCH, Aspen Publishers, and Kluwer Law International products. (www.WKLegaledu.com)

To contact Customer Service, e-mail customer.service@wolterskluwer.com, call 1-800-234-1660, fax 1-800-901-9075, or mail correspondence to:

> Wolters Kluwer
> Attn: Order Department
> PO Box 990
> Frederick, MD 21705

Printed in the United States of America.

1 2 3 4 5 6 7 8 9 0

ISBN 978-1-4548-4039-8

Library of Congress Cataloging-in-Publication Data

Names: Kamita, Jennifer, author. | Hawthorne, Christopher (Law professor), author. | Bensinger, Sascha, author.
Title: Exam first aid : multiple-choice exams / Jennifer Kamita, Clinical Professor of Law, Loyola Law School, Los Angeles; Christopher Hawthorne, Clinical Professor of Law, Loyola Law School, Los Angeles; Sascha Bensinger, Former Clinical Professor of Law, Loyola Law School, Los Angeles.
Description: New York : Wolters Kluwer, [2016]
Identifiers: LCCN 2016033528 | ISBN 9781454840398
Subjects: LCSH: Law–United States–Examinations, questions, etc. | Law examinations–United States. | Bar examinations–United States.
Classification: LCC KF388 .K36 2016 | DDC 340.071/1–dc23
LC record available at https://lccn.loc.gov/2016033528

SUSTAINABLE FORESTRY INITIATIVE | Certified Sourcing | www.sfiprogram.org | SFI-01028

About Wolters Kluwer Legal & Regulatory US

Wolters Kluwer Legal & Regulatory US delivers expert content and solutions in the areas of law, corporate compliance, health compliance, reimbursement, and legal education. Its practical solutions help customers successfully navigate the demands of a changing environment to drive their daily activities, enhance decision quality and inspire confident outcomes.

Serving customers worldwide, its legal and regulatory portfolio includes products under the Aspen Publishers, CCH Incorporated, Kluwer Law International, ftwilliam.com and MediRegs names. They are regarded as exceptional and trusted resources for general legal and practice-specific knowledge, compliance and risk management, dynamic workflow solutions, and expert commentary.

To our students

SUMMARY OF CONTENTS

CONTENTS

Introduction: How To Use This Workbook

"Professor, I need help with multiple-choice exams."

Over the years, we have heard this plea over and over from our students. Students come to our offices—often with otherwise impressive academic records—asking specifically for help with law school multiple choice exams. In response, we put together a systematic way to evaluate and improve our students' multiple-choice exam scores.

Based on our informal polling of students who have used this system, we can say one thing about it: It works. Students who have followed this system have measurably improved their multiple-choice scores on law school exams and on the Multistate Bar Exam (MBE).

Why does the system work? Well, possibly because it *is* a system. Most students have a system for taking an essay exam. At the very least, their thinking is structured by breaking down a fact pattern into issues and sub-issues, using the right rule, applying the rule to the facts, concluding, and moving on to the next issue. In other words, IRAC: IRAC is the system, or at least one system, for approaching an essay question.

What is astonishing is that few students come into our offices with a *system* for approaching a multiple-choice question or exam. Many students (and professors) seem to believe that multiple-choice exams simply evaluate a student's knowledge of the rules. Others think that the ability to excel at multiple-choice exams is instinctive and that a talented student who has studied hard will simply recognize the right answer without thinking too much. In other words, they think a multiple-choice exam is a *recognition* exam, not an *analysis* exam.[1]

Seeing these assumptions in print, you may already have noticed the problem with them. Because—of course—a law school multiple-choice exam is *analytical.* It isn't just scanning the answers and expecting one to call your name just because you studied so hard. Law school multiple-choice exams are 20, 40, or 100 discrete pieces of analysis. The fact that there is only one right answer (rather than a spectrum of good to excellent answers) makes the analysis harder, not easier.

It doesn't get easier on the MBE. It's harder. In fact, students who have muddled through multiple-choice exams in law school may first discover they have a problem with multiple choice *when* they take the MBE. If that's you, welcome: The system works for the MBE as well. The only difference is you're dealing with eight subjects,[2] not just one. Keep reading.

When a student enters our offices, we always ask questions about three problem areas. Each area has its own system. We try to figure out if the poor score is the result of (1) the student's time management, (2) the student's multiple-choice exam-taking skills, or (3) the student's problems with the substantive material itself. It could be only one problem; more frequently, it is some combination of two or all three. A problem with any *one* area will cause problems on the exam.

We generally ask students the following questions.

1. Did you finish the exam? And even if you did, were you comfortable with your timing? (Time management)

2. Tell me how you approach an exam question. What do you look at first? (Exam-taking skills)

3. Do you take practice exams? If so, tell me what you do when you get the wrong answer. (Substantive problems)

---

1. A recognition question asks, "What is the correct rule," while an analysis question asks, "How does the correct rule apply to these specific facts?"

2. The subjects tested on the MBE are civil procedure, constitutional law, contracts, criminal law, criminal procedure, evidence, property, and torts.

This workbook is organized around these three questions. But they are very general questions, and often give rise to sub-questions. That's why we include an expanded version of these questions below (the Self-Diagnostic Questionnaires or "SDQs"). We strongly suggest you go through the SDQs *before* you continue reading this book. When answering the questions, be honest and complete. While you shouldn't grope for things you're doing wrong (maybe you're doing something right!), you should be unsparing in your analysis of what you do before and during an exam.

Ready? Let's go!

PART ONE—TIME MANAGEMENT

Part One of this book deals with time management both before and during the exam. We break up time management into two discrete areas because each area requires a different set of time management skills. While there are more detailed versions of these questions in Chapter 1, for now, consider the following.

EXAM FIRST AID—SELF-DIAGNOSTIC QUESTIONNAIRE

Time Management

Before the Exam

1. Did you finish your substantive outlines?
2. Did you have enough time to test your outlines for accuracy on a practice exam?
3. Did you have enough time to memorize your outline?
4. Did you have enough time to test your knowledge on a practice exam?

During the Exam

5. Did you finish the exam?
6. Did you have enough time to correctly mark your Scantron[3]?
7. Did you have enough time to review only the questions where you were unsure of your answer?

If you didn't have time to finish your course outline, *if* you didn't have time to test the accuracy of your outline with practice exams, *if* you didn't have enough time to learn or memorize your outline . . .

   . . . *then* **you have a time management problem *before* the exam.**

---

3. Scantron supplies the majority of optical reader cards used on law school tests. If your school uses a different brand of card, mentally substitute its name instead. Because Scantron is now a brand name like "Kleenex" that carries a generic meaning, we use it throughout this book.

This problem will have an impact on your multiple-choice performance. You won't be able to readily identify the issue, recall the applicable rule or exceptions, separate the probable answers from the improbable ones, and finally, apply your knowledge to the probable answers to select the correct answer to the question. This problem is covered in Chapters 3, 4, and 5.

On the other hand, *if* you are rushing to finish the last few questions or you don't have time to review your answer choices on the questions where you were unsure of your answer . . .

. . . *then* you have a time management problem *during* the exam.

This problem will affect your multiple-choice performance because (as you have guessed) if you can't read and answer a multiple-choice question, you can't get credit for it. This problem is covered in Chapter 6.

It is not uncommon to have time management problems both before *and* during the exam. In fact, one problem may conceal another. If you have *any* time management concerns, read all of Part One.

SPECIAL NOTE TO BAR EXAM STUDENTS

The time management skills discussed in Chapters 3 through 5 are tailored specifically to the needs of law students. However, Chapter 6, "Time Management During the Exam," applies to both law school exams and state bar exams.

PART TWO—THE APPROACH

Part Two deals with actual multiple-choice exam-taking skills. It discusses how you should approach the reading of the question, narrowing down the answer choice to the probable answers, and dealing with being unsure of your answer. Consider the following.

EXAM FIRST AID—SELF-DIAGNOSTIC QUESTIONNAIRE

The Approach

Do you have an approach strategy for answering the question that allows you to

- narrow the issue(s) before reading the fact pattern;
- separate the possible answers from the improbable ones; and
- among the answers, distinguish between certain and uncertain answers?

If you already have a system that is a resounding success, then use that one. On the other hand, because a good system usually produces good results (and here you are, reading this book), the one you are using may not be working to your satisfaction. Try this one on several practice exams before deciding to return to your old one.

In fact, it is more likely that you have no system for answering multiple-choice exams. As we mention above, students often feel that they don't need a system because they've been doing multiple-choice exams their whole lives. But because a law school multiple-choice exam is based on analysis rather than recognition, you need a system. This system is covered in Chapters 8 through 11.

PART THREE—EVALUATING PERFORMANCE AND DIAGNOSING PROBLEMS

Part Three addresses how to look critically at your performance on a multiple-choice exam. Only by critically evaluating *why* you missed selecting the correct answer—and then correcting the problem—can you realistically hope to improve your multiple-choice performance. Consider the following.

EXAM FIRST AID—SELF-DIAGNOSTIC QUESTIONNAIRE

Evaluating Performance and Diagnosing Problems

Do you have a system[4] for evaluating your incorrect answer to determine whether the answer is incorrect because of

- reading problems,
- a lack of substantive knowledge, and/or
- confusion from using commercial materials?

Part Three will help you pinpoint your problems with the substantive material and improve your multiple-choice scores. Evaluating your multiple-choice exam-taking performance is the most time-consuming and detailed of the three parts. It has two steps: (1) determining whether you have a *reading* problem (that is, whether you are getting what you need in the test from the fact pattern and the answers), and (2) identifying and correcting substantive problems in your outline and rule memorization.

Of course, these two steps are interrelated. You need to know the law in order to spot the correct issues and answers in a multiple-choice question, and knowing the law but failing to read well enough to spot an issue or a sub-issue is a massive and frustrating waste of time. Therefore, going

---

4. Simply reading the correct answer and mentally noting why you missed the question is not a sufficient method to enable you to improve your multiple-choice scores. Making a mental notation and doing nothing more indicates a belief that you will forever remember the mistake you made and will not repeat it.

through one of the above steps usually helps you master the other step. Also, working on one area of evaluation may uncover problems with another area. One major concern (major enough that we devote a whole section in Chapter 22 to it) is the confusion that can result from using *general* commercial multiple-choice practice questions and outlines for your *specific* professor's multiple-choice exam.

What Part Three *won't* tell you is this: "All you need to do is work through 2,000 multiple-choice questions and you'll automatically get better." In our experience, that's not true. Practice is important, but if it were enough, the merely mule-headed would have a big advantage over the thinking student. Instead, Part Three will give you a systematic way to identify and deal with your problem areas. If you follow the system, it will help you identify the areas where you need to focus to improve your exam scores. This system is covered in Chapters 12-22.

In addition to Parts One, Two, and Three, the book also includes three appendices.

Appendix A—Exam First Aid—Self-Diagnostic Questionnaire

Appendix A is the basic handout we prepared for our students who come to us with multiple-choice exam problems. We do not recommend you start with this summary because it does not contain the examples and exercises that illustrate the points we are trying to make. It is, however, a useful tool to stay oriented once you understand what we are telling you to do.

Appendix B—Time Management Worksheets

Appendix B contains the worksheets, with instructions, that guide you through managing study time. Both weekly and monthly worksheets are included. The instructions are a condensed version of the instructions discussed in the text of Part One, Chapters 3 and 4.

Appendix C—Resources of Sample Multiple-Choice Questions with Explanatory Answers

We recommend that you read through the entire workbook at least once to identify the areas you need to work on. Once you have identified those areas, practice the skills on sample multiple-choice questions. We have included references to other resources where you can obtain practice questions with explanatory answers.

One final note: The system we recommend is complete—from time management to evaluating and correcting your areas of weakness to take that final multiple-choice exam. While we have had success with students who only use one or two of our recommendations, the greatest success come from students who use the entire system. In the beginning, you may find the system time consuming. But once you incorporate it into your routine, you will find that these skills will serve you well as you move through law school and later as you prepare for the bar exam.

EXAM FIRST AID
Multiple-Choice Exams

A Systematic Approach to Improving Multiple-Choice Performance

Part One
TIME MANAGEMENT

Evaluate how you spend your time before the test (preparation) and during the test.

Part Two
THE APPROACH

Create an exam strategy for choosing the right answer.

Practice Multiple-Choice Questions

Part Three
EVALUATING PERFORMANCE AND DIAGNOSING PROBLEMS

Make necessary changes to how you read the questions and/or learn the substantive material.

THE TEST

TIME MANAGEMENT

Overview

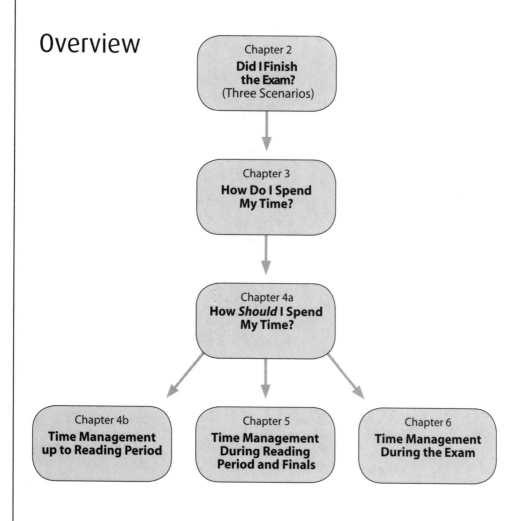

Chapter 2
**Did I Finish
the Exam?**
(Three Scenarios)

Chapter 3
**How Do I Spend
My Time?**

Chapter 4a
**How *Should* I Spend
My Time?**

Chapter 4b
**Time Management
up to Reading Period**

Chapter 5
**Time Management
During Reading
Period and Finals**

Chapter 6
**Time Management
During the Exam**

CHAPTER 1

How to Use This Part of the Book

"Well begun is half done."
—Aristotle, Politics

Some things are in abundant supply in law school: reading and writing assignments, stress, more stress, crazily intense fellow students, blows to your self-esteem. One item, however, always seems to be in short supply: time.[1] How well you manage this scarce resource will greatly influence how you feel during the semester and how you perform on exams.

Time management seems simple—as simple as the advice the grown-ups once gave you: "Stop dawdling! Focus! Get back to work! Turn off the television! You're going out *now*?" Of course, if we could put this "valuable" advice into practice just by listening to our elders, we wouldn't need books like this one. In fact, time management is difficult and requires thought, planning, and a healthy appreciation for your own frailties. We *all* have difficulty concentrating. Work is not always a pleasure. Recreation is essential.

It's hard to think about time management—it's a fairly elusive subject. Whenever you think about time management, you always want to think about the *thing* that is being managed: torts, criminal law, constitutional law. But time management is like the glue and screws that hold together your bed: largely invisible, but try getting a good night's rest on a bed that falls apart.

---

1. And, by extension, sleep.

Although time management is important, it's not easy. It's a *daily* commitment you make to your law school career. Some days you'll fulfill that commitment, other days . . . not so much.

You may be tempted to skip this chapter and jump ahead to where the "real" system begins. But multiple-choice exams, though they involve many skills, are basically about *time*. Three minutes per question. Two minutes per question. Careful reading and complicated thought in three minutes. In two minutes. In one-and-a-half minutes.

So why not just talk about *that* skill—micromanaging small pieces of time? Because you need to sweat the big stuff before you sweat the small stuff. Manage your time on a daily or a weekly level, and you'll manage your time better on the smaller scale of one, two, and three minutes.

Let's start with the biggest possible picture. Here are three things about time management to keep in mind.

Forgive your trespasses

One important piece of time management is being honest with yourself. Much ink has been spilled about how law school changes you, changes your thinking, and changes your personality. One thing, on the other hand, is *not* likely to change without Herculean effort: your studying style. Can you sit motionless for four hours, utterly absorbed in your casebook? If you can, thank your lucky stars, though you may want to check your ability to retain material during the last two hours. If you *can't* sit still for more than an hour, don't try to suddenly change your study style. Accommodate your working style to your *own* capacities, but anticipate the situations in which that working style may become a liability. For example, law school exams, like the bar exam, are given over several hours—two or three and sometimes even four hours. If you cannot sit with focused concentration for more than an hour, then you probably won't do very well. Gradually extend your study time until it feels (sort of) natural to sit still for long periods of time.

Despite all this conditioning, however, you should still try improve your study efficiency. But how? Virtue and conditioning alone will not avail you in the dark watches of the night. Which brings us to . . .

Be afraid...be a little afraid

The strange thing about time is that it's elastic. How many times have you looked up from a book and discovered you read for three hours when you only intended to read for one? On the other hand, how many times have you gotten up from your desk, feeling like three hours had passed, and found that less than an hour had gone by? Luckily, you already possess the oldest efficiency tool in the world: FEAR.

Remember how, at the beginning of the first semester, you spent endless amounts of time reading through a single case, while by the end of the semester, you could burn through a case in 15 minutes? While some of that speed was the product of mastery, a lot of it was plain old fear. You knew you were running out of time, and you focused accordingly, all the while thinking, why couldn't I do this at the beginning of the semester??

Cue: relaxing mood music. It is once again the beginning of the semester—the *second* semester. You have all the time in the world. Back to reading cases the way you read novels, taking notes in class and forgetting about them instantly, never missing a campus party, and putting off reading for another day—because, after all, it's the *beginning* of the semester, the sweet, indolent period of law school life.

Cue: ominous organ chords. Let's throw a few long, dark shadows across this pastoral scene ...

FINAL EXAMS ARE LESS THAN FOUR MONTHS AWAY

That's right. No matter which law school you attend, final exams are always right around the corner. Those exams—the ones that caused you so much pain last semester—are coming again. The time to start preparing is *now*.

Did you feel a tingle? Good. Whenever you feel complacent, whenever you feel like you have all the time in the world, look at the words above and remind yourself that you should be preparing for exams *all the time*.

Psychologists will tell you that, contrary to popular opinion, small doses of fear are not a bad thing. This is especially true for law students. Small doses of fear help rather than hinder your eventual success. The key word here is "small": "small" doses. Experiencing—and managing—small doses of fear now will help you deal with the massive doses of fear that will be your constant companions at the end of the semester.

To analogize, imagine you want to become the hot dog eating champion of the world in four months. To achieve your dream of being the world champion of hot dog eating,[2] you would want to start slowly, with four to five hot dogs at a sitting, working your way up to the maximum as the contest nears. It's the same with the management of fear: start small. Now is not the time to be overly motivated by fear; don't exhaust yourself. But don't ignore it either. You need more than an intellectual appreciation of what lies ahead—you need to feel it, however mildly, in your gut.

Time management is hardest at the beginning of the semester because of these two conflicting realities. First, the brief thrill of fear you felt when contemplating the reality of impending exams is already dissipating. Isn't it? On the other hand, when you *do* force yourself to think, it seems completely overwhelming. Four or five subjects! Countless cases! How long should my outlines be? Long? Short? Should I buy bootleg outlines from Ralph the Outline Salesman? What about that Guy on the Internet who will sell his Patented Study Method for a mere $49.95? Or maybe . . . I'll just think about it another day. Yeah. Sigh. Now I feel better.

Or perhaps you should think about it now, while you have this book in your hands. Let's take a few halting steps to overcome the inertia.

Break it up

You can break up the overwhelming task of time management into four different tasks, which we will term Micro, Macro, the Sprint, and Exam Day.

---

2. Currently, Joey "Jaws" Chestnut, though it is wise never to count out former world record holders Matt "Megatoad" Stonie and Takeru "Tsunami" Kobayashi.

Micro refers to your daily schedule: How much time do you have every day for studying, eating, sleeping, exercise, recreation, spiritual practice, and maintaining relationships? This will ensure that you leave enough time during the day to stay current on your reading, note-taking, outlining and taking practice exams.

Macro refers to how you plot out the full semester in a series of *deadlines*, counting back from the dates of your finals. This will ensure that you don't fall behind on important tasks such as filling in note holes, finishing your outlines, and testing your outlines with practice exams.

The Sprint refers to the two weeks before exams, when you will be juggling important tasks day by day and making sure you allocate sufficient time to each subject, while maintaining your optimum level of concentration.

Exam Day is what it sounds like: how to manage your time, and your mood, on the day of your exam, both before, during, and after the event. Many students manage the run-up to exams masterfully and then go kablooey on exam day. But time management is important on exam day, especially if you have other exams coming up. Having helped hundreds of students improve their scores over the years, we've noticed that it's very hard to help yourself when you have to start everything from scratch, and copying out charts and templates is pretty close to starting from scratch. Therefore:

- **Use the charts in the book.** Whether you create your own or use the online templates and charts, practicing immediately will help cement the lessons in your mind. If you think you'll do several drafts, then copy out the relevant parts or use the online templates.

- **Don't just read.** Some other books that teach you about study and exam techniques are just that: books. You curl up with them, and they offer comfort and entertainment. This is a workbook. It is designed to get you writing, planning, and preparing for multiple-choice exams *right now*.

- **Connect the tools to real situations.** As painful as it may be, think back to last semester (or back to the time before your most recent midterm) and connect your experience with the experiences we describe in the book. Otherwise, you will have no context for the tools in this book or may conclude that these tools are redundant or even useless. You may say, "I don't need to change anything. I just didn't try hard enough. I'll try harder next time." But "trying harder next time," by itself, is almost never enough to improve an exam score. Everybody tries hard in law school. You need to know what to try hard *at*. To do that, go back to the day (or the week) where you realized that the exam you were about to take was really, really hard, and you wish you had planned better and started everything earlier. Fix that in your mind. Feel the sharp needles of regret. Thanks, Professors!

FIRST, A FEW QUESTIONS ABOUT YOUR TIME MANAGEMENT

Answering the following questions will allow you to further pinpoint any time management problems. Be honest—after all, there's no one around but you. Once you have answered all of them, you will have a pretty good idea of which areas of time management you need to work on.

Before the Exam

1. How well did you use your time during the semester?

    a. In school or on school-related activities (e.g., class prep, outlining, practice exams)

    b. On non-school-related activities (e.g., job, family, friends)

2. Did you spend enough (or too much) time on class preparation?

3. Did you spend time after class correcting and/or reviewing your class notes and case briefs?

4. Did you spend enough (or too much) time working on your outlines?

5. Did you finish your outlines?

6. Did you have time to "test your outlines" to see whether they would work for you on an exam? If any outline did not work well, did you have enough time to correct your outline and then test it again?

7. Did you have enough time to learn/memorize your outline?

8. Did you have time to "test your knowledge" by taking practice exams?

During the Exam

9. Did you finish the exam?

10. Did you have enough time to correctly mark your Scantron[3]?

11. Did you have enough time to review only the questions where you were unsure of your answer?

Now, with your answers in mind, continue to Chapter 2 and think about how your time management translated into your experience on exam day.

---

3. Scantron supplies the majority of optical reader cards used on law school tests. If your school uses a different brand of card, mentally substitute its name instead. Because Scantron is now a brand name like "Kleenex" that carries a generic meaning, we use it throughout this book.

Did I Finish the Exam?
(Three Scenarios)

Before answering this question, consider your experience on your last multiple-choice exam. Merely getting all the questions answered isn't usually enough. "Finishing" means more than just filling in the bubbles on a Scantron form. Here are three possible scenarios:

Scenario 1

You finished the exam with enough time to

- work through all the problems with relative confidence in your answer choices, *and*

- correctly mark your Scantron form, *and*

- conduct a second (or third) review of only the questions where you were unsure of your answer and finish the exam satisfied with your answer choices.

If this describes your time management experience, congratulations! You do not have a time management problem, either before or during the exam. You can skip this chapter!

On the other hand, if you are reading this book, you are probably dissatisfied with your multiple-choice score, which means that your lightning-quick performance on the exam may have been the result of carelessness and hurry. If you use the techniques in this book to improve your exam-taking experience, you may find that you *don't* have the time to finish the test when you are actually reading carefully. In that case, circle back and ask these questions again.

Scenario 2

You finished the exam only because you simply gave up and guessed at the answers. Now you have a time management problem. The problem is not about how you managed your time *on* the exam but on how you managed your time *before* the exam. Quite frankly, if you were only guessing at the answers, then

- your outline was not detailed enough to answer the question, and/or

- you did not spend enough time learning the material, and/or

- you did not spend enough time taking practice exams.

At this point, you may be tempted to throw this book away, hurry back to the library to study, and take more practice exams. This is particularly tempting if you're reading this in a bookstore. But you're a law student: there's no question you're smart. It's safe to say that, if effort and inborn intelligence were enough to allow you to excel on a multiple-choice exam, you would have done so by now. Therefore, read on.

Scenario 3

You did not finish the exam, but *on the questions you answered,* you

- worked through all the problems with relative confidence in your answer choices, *and*

- correctly marked your Scantron, *but*

- did not have time to get to all the questions, *or*

- did not have time to conduct a second (or third) review of the question where you were unsure of your answer choice.

In this case, you have a time management problem *during* the exam and possibly *before* the exam because you were unable to quickly spot the issue, know the rule, and apply it to the facts to reach your conclusion (IRAC).

If, after reading the above, you're not sure whether you have a time management problem, turn the page. For better or worse, restructuring your time is best accomplished from the ground up, for two reasons: First, you need to know how much study time you really have before you can allocate study time. Second, "time suckers"—parasitical activities that siphon off valuable study time—often become clear only when you objectively look at your entire day.

Turning the page . . .

CHAPTER 3

How Do I Spend My Time?
(Every Day)

This next chapter may be *genuinely* optional.[4] If your time management problems are confined to multiple-choice exams—that is, you already study effectively for and excel on essay exams—then *skip* this part. Yeah, we really mean it. No, seriously. *Skip* it.

If, however, your concerns encompass more than just multiple-choice questions, then this part is for you. Preparing for multiple-choice exams is exactly like preparing for essay exams, at least in one respect: It takes *a lot* of time to learn the material, organize it, and practice using it in an exam setting.

You've probably heard this before, but for *each hour* of time you spend in a law school class, you should spend *at least* three to four hours per week outside of class studying. This means that 15 hours in class equals 45 hours per week of studying outside of class. Added together, you have 60 hours a week, which is the equivalent of one-and-one-half full-time jobs. That's 10 hours a day, six days a week, and that's the *minimum*. And your study schedule during exam time will encompass even *more* hours per week.

If this amount of studying seems too unfathomable to comprehend, then go back to the three precepts introduced in Chapter 1: (1) forgive your trespasses; (2) be afraid . . . be a little afraid; and, most important, (3) break it up.

---

4. **Special note to bar exam applicants:** The time management skills discussed in Chapters 3 through 5 are tailored specifically to the needs of law students. However, Chapter 6, "Time Management During the Exam," applies to both law school exams and state bar exams.

Naturally, although it's unpleasant to be in a state of fear, as we pointed out above, well-managed doses of fear can be very useful. The key words are "well-managed" and "doses." So the key to not being overwhelmed—that is, managing your fear—is to break up your task in the smallest practicable pieces. That process starts by looking at the Micro aspect of your schedule—what you do day in and day out, hour by hour. Then we'll find out just how forgiving you can be with yourself.

MICRO SCHEDULE: YOUR DAILY CALENDAR

To begin, however, let's not be forgiving. Much of what you may call "studying" is what an objective observer would call "messing around." So just to be clear:

Studying is defined as

1. class preparation,

2. legal research and working on your legal writing papers,

3. working on course outlines,

4. taking practice exams,

5. working in study groups, and

6. meeting with your professors to discuss the material.

Studying is *not*

1. "hanging out" on campus,

2. meeting with student groups (e.g., Student Bar Association, Environmental Law Society, Law Students for Serious Partying), or

3. socializing in the library, in the quad, after class, or anywhere else.

Appendix B provides a blank daily calendar template on which you can map out every waking (and sleeping) hour of your day, seven days a week.[5] Now, in *normal* life, you would not have to be this hyper-organized. If you are a person with a full-time job, you can expect to spend eight hours or more per day doing what your boss directs you to do. You can leave the weekends free because your obligations probably cease when you leave work. Food, sleep, laundry, and commuting get tossed in there somewhere, and of course, you have to see the family, which takes away from your valuable free time.

In law school, however, you are largely *self*-directed. Nobody will tell you to study, or to read this many cases per day, or to start outlining, or to start taking practice exams. And it's unrealistic—and a waste of time—to begin each day anew, bouncing out of bed and saying, "*What* shall I study today?" Better to externalize your inner boss and get your schedule on paper—and then *follow* that schedule. Better to know at every moment of the day where you really have to be than to experience a painful inner struggle every time you start to study, or to allow indecision to creep in and stop you before you even get started.[6]

One of the things that the daily calendar will reveal is how *little* time you have to study. Once you fill in the nonschool essentials: sleep, food, and errands—there's not much time left for everything else. So the "everything else" had better be something pretty good to drag you away from your books. Also, if you have too *much* "everything else," you need to ask yourself what part of "everything else" you can do without.

To plan your studies realistically, with the daily calendar:

First: For *each* day, mark the time you spend on the following activities.

- In class:

  - Don't forget to include the time immediately after class. This is often the best time to fill the gaps in your understanding.

---

5. See also the electronic charts at http://aspenlawschool.com/books/Kamita_Exam/.

6. One more reason: As a practicing attorney, you face an 80 percent chance that you will have to keep track of your time for billing purposes. Lawyers complain about this all the time—but get into the right habit early, and you can transform this chore from extremely painful to merely annoying.

- Taking care of *physical* needs. These include:

  ○ Eating: Make sure you block out time for meals.

  ○ Sleeping: Be realistic about the amount of sleep you need. Do *not* include sleep deprivation as part of your schedule.

  ○ Exercise: With this amount of studying, your metabolism slows down and gets very sluggish. Make sure you do something to keep moderately fit. Not *admirably* fit: The best-built lawyer rarely wins the case.

  ○ Hygiene: Not showering or brushing your teeth may indicate an admirable devotion to the law . . . or possibly just slovenliness.

- Taking care of *spiritual* needs. These include:

  ○ Religious services or activities

  ○ Meditation

  ○ Any other private form of worship or coping

  ○ It *may* include regular counseling.

- Taking care of *emotional* needs, like these:

  ○ Friends. Good to have in law school.

  ○ Relationships. Bad to start in your first year of law school (you have been warned), but good to keep if you already have one. If you are in a long-term relationship that is important to you, this should be at the top of your list, right after sleeping, eating and hygiene.

  ○ Relatives. Important—but of all people, they should be the most understanding of your need to excel in law school. "Relatives," of course, includes your child or children, if you have them. During law school, nobody is a full-time parent. But you can manage your available time so as to be a *good* parent. Whole books have been written on this, but in general, being a good parent is a lot like being a good lawyer: *commit* to a special time on a regular timetable, and *keep* that commitment. One nice distinction: you don't have to bill your child for time.

- Taking care of *mental* needs. This *does not* include *school*. It *does* include:

  ○ Recreational reading

  ○ Entertainment

  ○ Your deep, personal involvement with certain sports franchises

- Taking care of *financial* needs. These include:

  ○ Full-time work: If you are a full-time first-year law student, we recommend that you *not* work at a job during the school year. But if you are a part-time student, or are experiencing financial hardship, then you have to work. In that case, be realistic about how much time your job takes. Be honest with your supervisor. An overdemanding boss has hurt the academic career of many a law student.

  ○ Work-study: Again, full-time first-year law students should avoid work-study unless it's absolutely necessary to their financial aid packages. Too much is riding on your first-year grades to sabotage them with 10 hours of work on a job that you will not have in three years.

Second: Identify your study time.

- Here's the hard part. Once you have filled in those necessary blocks of time ("Do I *really* spend that much time eating?"), then look at the time you have left for studying.

- Block out your study times. Add up the number of hours. Again, remember that you need three to four hours per hour of class time *in addition* to class time. Then ask yourself:

"AM I COMFORTABLE WITH MY LEVEL OF COMMITMENT TO MY *GOAL* OF BECOMING A LAWYER?"

If not, now is the time to prioritize.

Third: Tips and comments to help you prioritize your time.

- Start by marking out the time allocations that are *not negotiable* (meaning, cannot be changed). This includes the following:

  ○ Commute time: Include the time it takes to get to the car or other transportation that gets you to school, along with jobs like shoveling out or brushing off the car if you live where it snows. You are "commuting" until you arrive at your destination.

  ○ Class time: Don't forget the time before class, during which you do a quick review of the material for the day. Include time after class in which you review your notes or ask the professor questions. Twenty minutes on either side should do it.

  ○ Sleep time: Calculate the amount of sleep you *normally* need. You will probably be on a different schedule during reading period and exam period. But at this time, do not try to "free" time by depriving yourself of sleep. Sleep deprivation has a cumulative effect. Being fatigued makes your brain foggy, and you become less efficient and more stressed about getting the work done, which makes you stay up later and deprive yourself of more sleep . . .

  ○ Work time: The time you spend at work (to satisfy your financial needs) may or may not be negotiable. Evaluate your financial situation and determine how many hours you really "need" to work. Law school is not the time to build up a nest egg—in fact, it may be a time for deficit spending because your earning power after law school (your ability to get a job) directly relates to your achievement in law school.

Then: Look at the time allocations that may be *negotiable*.

- Spiritual, emotional, and mental replenishment time. Everyone needs to engage in one activity that renews his or her energy. That one activity may be spiritual (going to church, mosque, or temple or simply meditating), emotional (being with family or friends) or mental (watching *Man vs. Wild*, reading Janet Evanovich novels, or doing the daily Sudoku puzzle, to name a few). The point is, you need to be sure to do something that renews your energy every week. Depending on how long the activity takes, you may be able to do it every day.

○ How much of your spiritual/emotional/mental health routine is really *essential*? If it takes up too much time, perhaps it has become a debilitating habit.

○ For example, if 15 to 30 minutes of recreational reading each night relaxes you and allows you to sleep better, then do it. But if you need to work out three hours at the gym per day (not including travel and clean-up time), that activity could probably be trimmed back.

Once you figure out how you spend your day, and how you *ought* to spend it, you need to place that day in the context of the semester, the quarter, or the other unit of time determined by your law school.[7] While your daily schedule may contain a five-hour block of time from 5:00 p.m. to 10:00 p.m. simply marked "studying," the *content* of those five hours will be determined by how close you are to exams.

MACRO SCHEDULE: YOUR WEEKLY/MONTHLY CALENDAR

For this, you need to have an idea of what your academic semester will look like at the *start* of the semester. By knowing what to expect during your semester, you can plan ahead.

Appendix B provides a blank monthly calendar template on which you can map out your semester. Here are some tips for using the monthly calendar to best advantage.

1. Start backward by calendaring information on your end-of-semester exams for each class. If possible, find out

   • the exam date,

   • the time,

   • the location,

---

7. The charts in this book assume a semester system.

- the type of exam (essay only, multiple choice only, or a combination), and

- if applicable, the weight of the exam (e.g., 25 percent midyear exam).

Knowing information about your exams will help you to prioritize your work.

For example, suppose your first exam at the end of the Fall 1L semester is a property final exam (worth 75 percent of the final course grade). Your second exam is a torts midyear exam (worth 25 percent of the final course grade). You should start working on your property outline first and spend more time on it. You will need to master property first, and the final exam is worth more than the torts midyear exam.

On the other hand, if the first exam is a property midyear exam (worth 25 percent of the final grade), but the second exam is a torts final exam (worth 75 percent of the final course grade), you should prioritize and plan your time differently. You should start working on your torts outline first and spend more time working on it, even though the first exam is in property.

2. Calendar dates of any midterm exams.

3. Calendar dates your legal writing papers are due.

4. Calendar dates of any ex-curricular workshops such as Academic Support outlining or exam writing workshops and substantive course review sessions.

5. Calendar school holidays and breaks.

MACRO AND MICRO CALENDARS WORK TOGETHER

Once you have completed your calendars, you will have, at a glance, an idea of what tasks need to be completed on a *weekly* basis. The monthly calendar, combined with your daily calendars (that identify your "study times") should enable you to identify the tasks that need to be completed as well as the order (prioritizing) of completing them.

Remember, while in law school, you are first and foremost a *law student*, and most of your time does (and should) go to the business of law school. If you're wondering whether you're up to this level of commitment, ask yourself again:

"AM I COMFORTABLE WITH MY LEVEL OF COMMITMENT TO MY *GOAL* OF BECOMING A LAWYER?"

Once you have decided your level of commitment, it's amazing how mature and focused you can be. You will probably astonish yourself.

CHAPTER 4

The Sequence of Study, or How *Should* I Spend My Time?

Okay, you've filled in your daily schedule, and now it is scattered with big blocks of time that read "Study." If you have been through one semester of law school, you know what to do with those blocks of time—but if you are underperforming on exams, then maybe there's something up with your study habits.

With an activity as prolonged and unstructured as study time, your habits are very important. And—being habits—they are largely unconscious. So, you may ask yourself, why on earth would I examine those habits? Answer: Don't bother, if they work for you. But if you don't *know* what works and what doesn't work, then you need to examine the components of your studying.

"Studying" in law school is basically a series of steps that starts with reading the cases and ends with the final exam. Do you have to do all the steps? No—not if what you are doing works for you. But if it doesn't, examining what you should be doing may give you clues to where your studying has gone awry.

A BASIC SEQUENCE OF STUDYING

Step 1

Read and brief the cases.

- Use whatever method seems appropriate for you, although your brief should focus on the basics: issue (phrased both narrowly and broadly), rule (both the general rule and any exceptions), analysis (the court's reasoning), and conclusion (the holding). (If you haven't yet learned how to brief cases using the IRAC or a similar method, you will!)

Step 2

Attend and participate in lectures.

- "Participate" doesn't mean you have to raise your hand and speak. If you're not comfortable with that, don't bother. It *does* mean that you should remain intensely *engaged* in class. Turn off Facebook, solitaire, and the Internet. Take notes. Write down everything the professor or a fellow student says *that's important*. Don't write down unimportant stuff. Listening and distinguishing between what's important and unimportant is a skill you are developing. Practice it.

Step 3

Correct your briefs.

- Your rule for battery was "The harmful or offensive touching of another person, with intention, without consent." That's a good rule. But your professor's rule is "Battery occurs when the defendant (1) acts volitionally and (2) intentionally (3) to cause harmful or offensive touching or the imminent apprehension thereof and (4) such touching does occur." She doesn't even mention consent. Which rule is correct? The professor's—by definition. Correct your brief.

Fill in your note holes.

- A "note hole" is what it sounds like—a gap in your class notes, which occurs when you are called on, when you get confused, or when you just space out. Don't wait until the end of the semester to fill these in. Corral a classmate; ask your professor. Copy someone else's notes. It really doesn't matter how you get the knowledge, as long as the holes get filled before you forget where the holes are.

Attend your professor's office hours to clear up any confusion.

- One of the most noticeable differences between successful and unsuccessful law students is this: Successful students go to office hours. But don't go unprepared. Bring a list of specific questions. Work out a tentative answer to the problem that confuses you. Be intellectually flexible—if the professor thinks that your fairly basic question is a gateway to an interesting policy problem, then listen. But don't forget to get your question answered at the end. One more bonus: Students who go to office hours find it easier to obtain references.

A Note About Step 3

Don't skip this step! While it may be tempting to dive straight to outlining, think about this: If the "raw materials" to create the outline are comprised of incorrect briefs and lecture notes with holes, the outline will be just as bad. Remember—garbage in; garbage out.

Step 4

Outline the course materials.

- When do you start to outline? Answer: As soon as your professor has finished lecturing on an information module.

  For example, in Contracts, "offer" is an information module. Once your professor has finished lecturing on "offer," you will have 95 percent of what you need to know about that issue. The other 5 percent comes from the interplay between offer and other contract issues, such as acceptance. Another way to look at an information module is as a *functional* subject area that you will use in answering an exam question. For example, "offer" is a functional subject area because, on an exam, you want to consider *all* possible aspects of offer before moving on to the issue of acceptance.

On the other hand, "strict liability and negligence in the late nineteenth century," while a useful historical or intellectual subject area, likely will *not* be a section of your outline.

Step 5

Test your outline on a practice exam.

- Because this book is a multiple-choice book, the "practice exams" we discuss are multiple choice. But testing your outline should be done early and often, both for multiple-choice and essay exams.

- Furthermore, although this is a multiple-choice book, nearly all law school exams have an essay component—which means your outline needs to serve double duty. So test your outline on both multiple-choice and essay exams.

- Make sure you choose a practice exam with an answer. For essay exams, you need a good sample answer. For multiple choice, the best tests are the ones with *explanatory* answers. Appendix C contains a list of sources for multiple-choice questions.

- For this step, don't memorize your outline. Instead, take the exam, untimed, with your outline next to you. Consult the outline for rules and examples. Check your work.

  The purpose of this exercise is to see whether the outline *works*—that is, *if* you had memorized it, would you have done well using it?

- The additional benefit is that you took an exam, following the intellectual structure you will use on the real exam. Your ideal exam experience, speeded *way* up, should feel like this one. Hold onto that feeling in the weeks and months ahead.

Step 6

Assess your outline—did it work for you?

- Now, don't just put the exam answers away. After taking a breather (wait overnight), take out the materials again. Look at the questions, your course outline, and your answers. Be systematic. Looking at your outline, consider the following:

  - Could you spot the issue?

  - Were your rules complete, clear, and concise?

  - Did you have enough facts and hypotheticals to know how to complete the analysis—both argument and counterargument?

  - Were your policy arguments placed where you would naturally raise them on an exam?

  - If applicable, were your issues raised in the proper sequence? (Organization)

- Now—here's the most important step. If the answer to all of these questions is "yes," then great! Move to Step 7. If the answer to any of the questions is "no" or if you were confused about an area of law, *now* is the time to see your professor. *Now* is the time to go back to Step 4 and revise your outline.

Step 7

About a month before the exam, start to memorize your outline.

- No, don't memorize everything in your outline. Memorize the *rules*. *Study* the supporting facts and examples.

- Don't take too long memorizing your outline. A common mistake students make is to wait and wait . . . and then take practice exams only the day before the test. Give yourself a hard deadline to take your first timed practice exam, and then take it whether you're ready or not.

Condense your outline.[8]

- By now, you know better what is and is not important. Shearing away superfluous doctrines and examples will clear your mind.

Combine issues with other issues on your outline.

- By now, you also know that certain issues, doctrines, and defenses go together like peanut butter and jelly.

  o A few examples:

    - Torts: Assault, battery, and intentional infliction of emotional distress often arise from the same facts. What are the differences?

    - Criminal law: Any time two people plan something, look for conspiracy, accomplice liability, and felony murder.

    - Property: An unsuccessful adverse possessor can sometimes get a prescriptive easement—a use right, rather than a possessory right.

Step 8

Test your knowledge on a practice exam.

- Take this exam under timed conditions and without your outline. You are now testing your knowledge, not your outline.

- If you find gaps in your knowledge, go back to Step 6. Assess your outline and your answers. Same problems as before? Or when you solved the old problems, did new ones come up?

- Don't stop with one practice exam—even if you feel satisfied with your performance on this one, take *at least* two timed exams.

- Do *not* take a full timed exam (either multiple choice or essay) the night before the actual final. If you know the substantive area where your knowledge is weak, do some multiple-choice questions in that area. Alternatively, if you cannot find multiple-choice questions on

---

8. For essay questions, prepare an exam checklist of issues. Condensing your outline into a one- or two-page checklist can give you a better feel for the shape of your exam answer.

that topic, find a couple of short hypotheticals on that topic and IRAC them to see how the issue, rule, and application come together.

OVERLAPPING AND MULTITASKING
(or "How do I do all this at the same time?")

Multitasking is something you know how to do, right? After all, you study, listen to music, watch the game on TV, and text your friends, all at the same time.

Nonetheless, studying several subjects at once, or studying different aspects of the same subject during the same period, seems to confound law students. But that's what you have to do if you hope to keep up with your exam preparation. One thing you have probably learned in law school—it doesn't help to leave things for the last minute.

Again, if you hope to do this by instinct, you may turn out all right. But if you want to examine your sequence of study and which components may not be working, you'll need to take it apart and look it over.

It is absolutely certain that in law school, you will be doing four or five things during the same period of time, *per subject.* Staying up-to-date on your exam preparation requires it. But it doesn't have to be confusing, as long as you know *what* you are doing, at what time.

For example, let's examine Contracts. Although more and more professors begin their Contracts classes by discussing offer and acceptance, a fair number still start with consideration, one of the strangest and most difficult concepts in law. So here you are in Contracts. Starting a *week before class,* you are briefing the cases (Step 1). Starting with the *first week of class,* you are participating in class and taking notes (Step 2). If you are staying on top of your tasks, you are also filling in note holes and asking questions right after the lecture (Step 3). Once the professor is done lecturing on the topic of consideration, you start outlining (Step 4), maybe by the *third week of class.*

This progression is illustrated in Table 4-1. Imagine that each box going across represents one week; four boxes represent one month.

Table 4-1. Example: Contract Formation

	Week Before School	Week 1	Week 2	Week 3	Week 4	Week 5	Week 6	Week 7	Weeks 8+	Reading Period
Consideration	Step 1	Steps 2 & 3	Steps 2 & 3	Step 4	Step 5	Step 6				Steps 7 & 8
Offer			Step 1	Steps 2 & 3	Step 4	Step 5	Step 6			Steps 7 & 8
Acceptance				Step 1	Steps 2 & 3	Step 4	Step 5	Step 6		Steps 7 & 8
Defenses					Step 1	Steps 2 & 3	Steps 2 & 3	Step 4	Step 5, etc.	Steps 7 & 8

Assuming that consideration is the first subject area taught, by the first week of school, you are actively participating in lectures and filling in note holes on consideration. Easy?

Well, wait. At the end of week 2, your professor is done with consideration. She's on to offer and then acceptance. And in week 3, you're briefing acceptance while you're participating in class and filling in note holes on offer. And because the professor's done with consideration, it's time to start outlining that piece of the course. And soon, when you're finishing off acceptance, you can test your consideration outline with a hypothetical—while you begin to outline offer. Multiply that by five classes and you have a serious organizational task.

Sounds crazy? However, if you look at a successful lawyer, you'll see that same sequence of preparation. The successful lawyer is interviewing clients and mulling over taking case D while she drafts the answer for case C, supervises discovery on case B, and goes to a settlement conference on case A. While you're at it, multiply those cases by five. Or ten.

So learning how to break down your study time into smaller tasks will help you stay on track—and if you are leaving out any of these steps, you may have found a study problem.

Using a subject template, like the Torts example in Table 4-2, break down your own classes into discrete subject areas and study tasks by numbering the boxes appropriately. It's not important that you spend the same amount of time on each task or that the tasks overlap the way they do in the table. It *is* important that you use the table to mark off each task as you finish it. Look at the Torts example and then try it out. The goal, more than anything else, is to have nothing but Step 7 (memorizing your outline) and Step 8 (testing your knowledge) left to do about a week before and during reading period.

Table 4-2. Example: Torts

Topic	Week Before School	Week 1	Week 2	Week 3	Week 4	Week 5	Week 6	Week 7	Weeks 8+	Reading Period
Intentional Torts—Causes of Action	Read & brief cases.	Read & brief cases. Participate in lecture. Correct briefs & notes.	Participate in lecture. Correct briefs & notes.	Outline materials.	Outline materials.	Test outline with practice exams.	Assess outline.			Memorize & condense outline & test your knowledge
Intentional Torts—Defenses			Read & brief cases.	Participate in lecture. Correct briefs & notes.	Outline materials.	Test outline with practice exams.	Assess outline.			Memorize & condense outline & test your knowledge.
Negligence—Breach				Read & brief cases.	Read & brief cases. Participate in lecture. Correct briefs & notes.	Participate in lecture. Correct briefs & notes.	Outline materials.	Test outline with practice exams.	Assess outline.	Memorize & condense outline & test your knowledge.
Negligence—Causation						Read & brief cases.	Participate in lecture. Correct briefs & notes.	Outline materials.	Test outline with practice exams.	Memorize & condense outline & test your knowledge.

CHAPTER 5

The Sprint: Time Management During Reading Period and Finals

Okay, you're down to the last two weeks. This is when you used to do *all* your studying.[9] Now, assuming you have managed your time wisely, all you have left to do is the final memorization of rules, factors, and terms of art (Step 7) and practice exams and hypotheticals (Step 8).

How you break up your time during reading period and exams should depend on a strict mathematical rule, viewed in light of three factors and then tweaked based on the special considerations below.

First, consider this rule.

RULE: ALLOCATE THE SAME AMOUNT OF TIME TO EACH EXAM.

- This assumes that all the exams have the same point value. If they do, no one subject is more valuable than another. Don't study the subject most that you love the most. Don't avoid the subject you hate.

- Ideally, study in three- or four-hour blocks, because that's how long exams are in law school. If you are one of those people who can't sit

---

9. Back in that innocent time we call "college days."

still that long, then study in three- or four-hour blocks with *brief* and *strictly limited* breaks.[10] (Remember when we said to forgive your own trespasses? You need to push yourself *realistically*. These strictly limited breaks should be no more than 10 minutes while studying and shrink to no more than 60 seconds during actual exams.)

- Stay with what you know. Don't change study habits or partners just for exams. If you have been successfully studying with a study group all semester, stick with it. If you've been studying alone, don't join a group. Don't change where you study, provided it allows you uninterrupted time. On the other hand, if you're one of those people whose eyes glaze over when you're in one place too long, then switch every three to four hours.

- Write it down! Use the calendars in this book and break up your days accordingly. We know a number of students who color-code their days during reading period. Monday is a blue-red-purple day, which means four hours on torts (blue), four hours on contracts (red), and four hours on constitutional law (purple). Once you have color-coded your days, follow the codes.

Second, consider these three factors.

1. What percentage of your final course grade does the exam represent?

   - When considering this, be utterly cold-blooded. If a certain exam counts for *all* of your grade and the rest count for only *half* of your grade, then study roughly *twice* as long for the first exam—assuming the courses' credit values are the same.

2. How did you do on the midterm?

   - If you had difficulty on the midterm in a particular subject, you will need to devote *more* time to that subject. Don't be vague about

---

10. If you are time-accommodated, then make your adjustments according to the actual time of your exams.

this—schedule more time, *in writing*, and then adjust if you are learning slower or faster than you expected.

3. Is the final exam cumulative?

   - If you don't know, ask your professor. If the exam is cumulative, you will need extra time to relearn material from last semester. If you did not do well on the midterm, you may be learning that material (practically) for the first time. Moreover, if the exam is cumulative *and* your midterm outline was deficient, you will need to build in time to correct that outline as well as to prepare a functional outline for the current semester.

Finally, consider the tweaks. These are idiosyncrasies that you may be able to anticipate, and not freak out over, when they come to pass. Accordingly, when using the calendars to plan your study time, consider these factors.

1. What your professor did:

   a. If your professor covered new substantive materials right up to the last day of class, you won't be finished with your outlines by the beginning of reading period—that's *normal*.

      - Plan to finish your outlines and test them (before memorizing them) as soon as possible.

   b. If your professor spent time reviewing substantive materials before reading period—

      - First, *attend* the review sessions.

      - Ideally, your outlines are already finished and tested. Use your professor's review to double-check the accuracy of your outlines.

      - Check your outline! For each topic, make sure

         ○ *I*— the outline covered the issues discussed in the review session,

         ○ *R*—the rules are written the way your professor wants them stated, and

         ○ *A*—the application section contains the arguments/policies discussed.

2. Create your game plan for finals:

   a. Be flexible, but remember that things generally take longer than you expect them to. If you find that you are underestimating your study time for each subject, then use self-sticking notes on your calendar so that you can easily revise your projections.

   b. Take advantage of what your professor is willing to do for you. For example, if your professor is willing to read practice essay exam answers, get your answers to him or her in enough time to make the professor's comments meaningful to you—in short, in enough time to make the corrections on your outlines and in your head.

   With multiple-choice exams, your professor may be willing to provide you with practice multiple-choice questions or recommend a specific source for practice multiple-choice questions. Your professor may even be willing to explain to you why a particular answer is correct and the others are not. You won't know what your professor is willing to do to help you prepare for the exam unless you ask!

   c. Test your outlines *before* you memorize the rules. You don't want to waste time memorizing incorrect information.

   d. Pace yourself from now until reading period so that you work hard but stay healthy. It is too soon to practice sleep deprivation.

CHAPTER 6

Exam Day

The Big Day Is Here(!)

Face it: Exam day isn't fun. It's not like graduation day, wedding day, or birthday. It's not a day of celebration—so looking forward to it, getting butterflies and goose bumps and all the other anticipatory reactions you get on days you actually look forward to—those are *bad* reactions. Ideally, exam day should be like any other day. Not a "big" day. Not even a medium-sized day.

"But what about adrenaline?" you ask. "What about that surge that helps me do my best and creates a satisfying sense of exhaustion after the exam?" Oh, please. No matter how calm you *intend* to be on exam day, you will never be so relaxed that you just sleep through the exam. No—the *good* adrenaline will be there no matter what. It's the *bad* adrenaline—the kind that makes you confused, scared, sleepy, roaring mad, and hung over, all at the same time—that you are trying to avoid.

So *if* . . .

- you have used your days well, studying instead of "studying," being systematic, pacing yourself and getting enough sleep;

- you have managed your time well during the semester, briefing and outlining on schedule, and starting on practice exams early enough to get the benefit from them;

- you have used the reading period intelligently, using a reliable system to practice and evaluate your performance; and

- you have a strategy for the exam that you have worked out and practiced beforehand;

... *then* your exam day should be merely unpleasant, like your average root canal—not horrendous, like diving into a tank full of piranha.

This chapter covers the fourth bullet point in the list above: creating an exam strategy. Fortunately, exam strategy for multiple-choice exams is simpler than essay exam strategy, for the same reasons that the exam itself is difficult: Multiple-choice exams are broken into small, equal parts. Each part generally has the same value. If you can do simple addition and division, you can create an exam strategy.

Before you do that, here are three things to remember about exam strategy.

1. **Never do anything for the first time in an exam.**

   Exams are about practice and preparation. So—*anything* you plan to do in an exam should be practiced beforehand. This includes (of course) practicing multiple-choice questions. But it also includes which materials you bring in, the layout of your materials at your workstation, the type of timepiece you bring in, whether you boot up your computer before you walk into the exam room or after, whether you wear earplugs (and which kind), and a host of other strange rituals. Walk through every step of the exam before the exam itself so that you face as few surprises as possible. Don't worry—there's always something you didn't anticipate.

2. **If there is something you can do before (not during) the exam, do it.**

   If you're lucky, your professor will tell you how many multiple-choice questions will be on the exam and how long you will have. In that case, figure out your time allocation for each question beforehand, memorize it, and write it down as soon as you are told to begin.

Of course, memorizing rules through mnemonics or anagrams is another way of completing work before the exam. Again, the general rule is if you *know* it's coming, figure out your response before it actually comes.

3. **Do *not* change your strategy in the middle of the exam.**

It is very tempting to get a "brilliant" idea for a change of strategy in the middle of an exam. Do not succumb to temptation. First—practice your strategy, so that you are invested in it. That will make you more likely to stick to it. Second, have a plan B already worked out. For example, if you find yourself falling behind, have a method for recalculating your strategy so you finish the exam on time.

It is very easy to be taken out of your game plan by fellow students. A chance remark from a classmate as you walk into the exam room can cause this. Your mind is racing, your emotions are raw, and you immediately think, "Crap, I've been doing it all wrong! *That* way sounds so much better. I have to switch!" Uh uh. Don't switch. Not during this exam.

Okay, now you're in the exam room: materials at the ready, earplugs in place, back straight, eyes forward, rules playing in your head like radio static. Dial it down, and do some simple strategizing.

CREATE YOUR EXAM STRATEGY

Step 1

Before reading any questions or marking any answers on the exam, *scan the entire exam* to determine how to allocate your time. Base this determination on

- the types of questions (e.g., multiple choice, essay, true/false),

- the number of questions,

- if indicated, the time allotted for each question, and

- if indicated, the weighted value for each question.

Once you have done that, *mark* your time allocation for the exam at reasonable intervals. Mark the time allocation directly *on the exam* itself. Use the time allocations to pace your work.

Consider the following example: Assume you have to answer 100 multiple-choice questions in two hours. Your exam starts at noon and ends at 2:00 p.m. You'll be doing 25 questions in half an hour, or a little more than a minute per question. It's a fast exam—but it's fast for everyone, so don't panic. Remember: You have a system!

Before beginning to answer the questions, mark on your exam as follows:

At question 25, write **12:30 p.m.**

At question 50, write **1:00 p.m.**

At question 75, write **1:30 p.m.**

At question 100, write **2:00 p.m.**

Make sure to write these notes in *large letters*, preferably in a brightly colored ink. You don't want to miss your strategy notations.

Now it may seem like a good idea to make more notations with shorter intervals—say, every 15 minutes. Unless the exam itself is less than an hour, that's not a good idea. Some questions will be harder; others you'll breeze through more quickly. On average, you can expect to reach question 25 in 30 minutes, but if the first 10 questions are really hard, you may find that you're 4 minutes behind at the 15-minute mark. Needless panic may set in, making it hard to remain analytical. So use this general rule: For exams more than one hour, use 30-minute intervals. For exams less than one hour, use 15- or 20-minute intervals.

Please note: This time strategy assumes you are marking your Scantron as you answer each question and do not need time to review your answers. If you need extra time to perform tasks such as marking your Scantron at the end or to review questions where you were unsure of your answer choice, *change your exam strategy* to account for the time.

Step 2

Always stick to your time allocations.

In the example above, when you come to question 25 in the exam, check your time. If you are at 12:30, you are on track. If you are at 12:35, you need to pick up speed. If you are at 12:20, you can slow down.

Again, pick up speed or slow down *deliberately*. If you reach question 25 at the 12:35 mark, you don't need to panic: You've been taking 84 seconds (1 minute 24 seconds) to do a multiple-choice question you need to do in 72 seconds (1 minute 12 seconds). While the seconds do add up, you need to go only about 10 to 15 percent faster—not twice as fast.

That's it!

(We said it was simple.)

A Note About the Multistate Bar Exam

When you are studying for the multistate bar exam (MBE), realize that some subjects have longer (more factually dense) questions than other subjects. For example, property questions tend to be fairly lengthy as compared to evidence questions. If you are taking a practice exam with property questions only, this time management system will probably not work because of the length of the questions. However, on the MBE itself, the seven subjects[11] are mixed—meaning that a property question may be next to a tort question followed by a contracts questions. You are unlikely to have three to four property questions in a row. When the lengthy questions (like property) are mixed with shorter questions (like evidence or criminal law), this timing system will work.

---

11. The seven MBE subjects are constitutional law, contracts, criminal law, criminal procedure, evidence, property, and torts.

KEEPING YOUR FOCUS

As we mentioned above, classmates, friends, and "frenemies" can be distracting, both before and after the exam. So a few words of advice about the prologue and the aftermath of exams:

Before the Exam

- Arrive on campus at least an hour before the scheduled time of the exam. If you have a long commute, take that into account. Check the traffic maps on the Internet if they are available.

- Consider whether studying in the library before exams is the best choice for you. The library can be like the ninth circle of hell before an exam. The panic and despair (of people who—unlike you—have not read this book, have not managed their time well, and have not developed an exam strategy) can be infectious. And while we would love you to recommend this book, you are probably better off studying—and right before an exam, the library can be a perilous place in which to do that.

- If it relaxes you to chat with friends outside the exam room, go ahead. But if you find that your classmates just cause you panic by asking you questions, engaging in gallows humor, showing off their voluminous knowledge, or having minor nervous breakdowns, then politely excuse yourself, go somewhere else, and keep focusing.

- Think twice before sitting with your best pal. Again—if you are sensitive to the emotions of others, and your friend is having a bad exam day (or an annoyingly good one—the kind punctuated by whoops of "I got it!" and "Score!"), then find another seat or even another room. You can always talk after the exam.

- Similarly, if you know that someone in your class is a particularly noisy breather, drums his fingers while thinking, laughs knowingly at the fact pattern, or types dizzyingly fast—this is not the time to be broad-minded. Avoid, avoid, avoid.

After the Exam

- Many a nerve has been shattered by hanging out on the quad after an exam is over and talking with fellow students about what was (and wasn't) on the test. Even your best friends can ruin your day just by saying, "Did you spot the defamation issue in the second question?" Of course, you didn't spot it—it wasn't there. But now you've given yourself something awful to think about for the next three weeks.

- Especially if you have more exams, walk to your car, your apartment, or a place of sanctuary, and avoid talking about the exam. It's past. There is nothing more you can do about it.

- If you do plan to get together with friends after exams, make a pact that *none* of you will talk about the issues, the questions, or anything else. Make it a rule that the first person to mention any specifics about the exam buys everyone else dinner that night. And make sure that person is not you—dinner can be expensive.

- Once you *do* get your exam back, even if you have done much better than before, don't stop evaluating, improving, and practicing. There's no telling how much better you can do, and every improvement will be reflected in your job opportunities and your life as a lawyer.

CHAPTER 7

A Final Note on Time Management

We realize that all this information is really hard to absorb—so don't try to put everything into practice at once.

Take the process step by step. Plan out your semester on the charts and calendars, and then use them to see how well they work. At times, the whole process will seem overwhelming. When that happens, take a deep breath and focus solely on the next small task, and then the one after that. Law school is such an irrational enterprise that if we had actually thought about the whole thing beforehand, we never would have gone at all. Exams are the same—if you actually thought about going through three to five grueling exams, you would probably go and pull the covers over your head. So don't think about the big picture: Use the charts and calendars and think about each task as it comes along.

That said, you should view the next few chapters in the context of this one. Working on your multiple-choice skills *must* rest on a foundation of good study habits and time management. So if you find that the system we outlined isn't working, page back to Chapter 1 and ask whether your skills rest on a shaky foundation.

A Systematic Approach to Improving Multiple-Choice Performance

Part One
TIME MANAGEMENT
Evaluate how you spend your time before the test (preparation) and during the test.

Part Two
THE APPROACH
Create an exam strategy for choosing the right answer.

Practice Multiple-Choice Questions

Part Three
EVALUATING PERFORMANCE AND DIAGNOSING PROBLEMS
Make necessary changes to how you read the questions and/or learn the substantive material.

THE TEST

THE APPROACH

Overview

```
Chapter 8
Using The
Approach
```

↓

```
Chapter 9
Scanning the Call of the
Question and the
Answer Choices
```

↓

```
Chapter 10
Reading the
Fact Pattern
```

↓

```
Chapter 11
Choosing
the Answer
```

Using The Approach

"It is enough if one tries merely to comprehend a little of the mystery every day."

—Albert Einstein

Before you read any further, first make yourself a promise: that you'll read through to the end of the chapter and that you will attempt to use the *entire* "Approach" for answering multiple-choice questions *before* you try to use pieces of it. Because the components fit together, one step may not be as effective if you don't go through the step before or after it. Don't question why each step exists, at least not yet. Follow the steps and see whether they work for you. They work for most students just the way they are.

The Approach is our system for attacking a multiple-choice question, no matter its content. It's the same for every question. When you use the same simple mechanical approach for every multiple-choice question, your mind is free to dwell on the more complex legal problems, which are *not* the same in any two questions.

Once you master The Approach, we encourage you to personalize it. You may find out you don't need to mark up the answer to the extent we recommend. Maybe you will figure out a unique approach to choosing the answer that allows you to shave seconds off your time for each multiple-choice question. If you've tested your own techniques and they work better than ours, then use them. Keep in mind, however, that it's much easier to create your own system when you already understand—thoroughly—another system.

"Wait, can I SKIP this part? Whaaaat?"

Chances are, if you're reading this book, you don't have an approach strategy that works for you. But if you do, test its usefulness by answering these questions:

> Does your approach strategy allow you to
>
> - narrow the issue(s) before reading the fact pattern;
> - separate the possible answers from the improbable ones; and
> - among answer choices, distinguish between certain and uncertain answers?

How do you know whether you meet those criteria? Well, the first thing you should look at is the score on your last multiple-choice test. You'll need two pieces of information:

1. Your raw score (number of questions correctly answered divided by total number of questions)

2. The mean score in your class.

Once you know these two pieces of information, you can figure out where you are in relation to the mean.

- If you are *well above* the mean (more than one standard deviation, or roughly in the 85th percentile or higher), then you are doing well. It would not be helpful—and might be harmful—to adopt a completely new system when you have one that is already working. But consider using Part Three to help you diagnose any remaining concerns. In fact, if you have isolated, sporadic problems, using the method in Part Three can be particularly helpful.

- Here's one example.

  ○ Your raw multiple-choice score is 15 out of 20, so you got 75 percent of the questions right. So you do have a basic understanding of doctrine, or you wouldn't have gotten that many correct.

- ○ The problem is, the mean score in your class was 15.88, which shows the test was a little too easy. Your score of 15 puts you below the mean, so in a class of 100 students, 50 to 60 students got better scores than you. In other words, you are in the 40th to 50th percentile in your class.

- ○ You can also expect that, in the second semester, your professor—seeing that lots of students did pretty well on the test—will make the test harder. That means your task will be more difficult, and for that, you'll need a system.

- Here's another example.

  - ○ Different test, and this time you got 9 out of 20, which makes you think you need a crash course in the black letter law. That may be—but wait until you look at the mean.

  - ○ And a good thing you did! The mean is 7.3, which shows the test was very, very hard. Your score put you in about the 85th percentile, which is very respectable.

  - ○ Keep in mind, however, that an answer or two either way could be very significant. Two more wrong, and you could be below the mean. Two more right, and you could be at the top of the class. If you hope to replicate or improve this result, you—again—need a system.

- Make sure, by the way, that you examine your multiple-choice scores for every class. A really good score in one class may mask structural problems with your overall approach. One really bad score may be an anomaly—though correcting that anomaly may mean you need to review your system for taking multiple-choice exams.

On the other hand...

If you're reading this book, chances are that you aren't happy with your multiple-choice approach. Or maybe you have *no* approach, and you think you just got lucky with the last couple of tests.

In that case, test this system out. It may be that you have a system, but you just haven't examined it sufficiently to figure out that it *is* a system. In that case, adopting this system—temporarily—may clarify your own system and possibly add a couple of useful components.

Okay . . .

You're about to read The Approach. When you read it, you may say "That's *it*? That's the approach I've been anticipating for all these pages?" And you'd be right: The Approach *is* simple. It's designed as a tool to manage the complex task of dealing with your multiple-choice concerns. And like most tools, it's versatile. Don't worry—you can supply the complication.

The Approach is simple because multiple-choice exams are high-stress affairs. During times of high stress, your choosing mechanism starts to freeze up. You have a hard time reading and thinking. You make choices not because they are the best ones, but because they are the simplest ones. You miss details. You misread sentences because your understanding of grammar becomes crude.

That's why a *system* is so valuable during high-stress situations. With a system, instead of making every decision *during* the situation, you make a number of general decisions *before* the situation arises. If I encounter something like *this*, I'll do *this*. Because I know *this* will almost certainly happen, I will prepare for it with *these* three steps. And if you know you're going to face a situation in which you will do roughly the same thing over and over, you can develop a strategy for dealing with the repetitive portions of the situation.

Here's a useful illustration of how having a system reduces the stress of taking a multiple-choice exam:

You are a simple cantina keeper on the planet Mos Def, and your town has been overrun by space pirates. One such space pirate, named Boba Tee, is chasing you through the white, lumpy buildings of your village— buildings that you once thought were dull and suburban but that now take on an ineffable poignancy, which you suspect is brought on by the fact that you may never see them again in this, our life.

Boba Tee is armed with a light saber, which he "borrowed" from a down-on-his-luck Jedi. Earlier, Boba demonstrated what a light saber could do to an ordinary grapefruit, and you want no part of that sizzling blade, so you are running away. You are faster than Boba (he wears the regulation lead-soled zero gravity space boot), and that's good. But you are tired, and you're not armed. You are about 10 feet ahead of him and out of range of his light saber. For the moment.

You can (a) flee across the wide plaza 50 feet to the left, zigzagging as you run; (b) shimmy up the lamppost coming hard on your right, hoping to climb out of range; (c) run down the narrow alley directly in front of you, which is perhaps 30 feet long and disappears into the murk; or (d) run into a curving street to your right, which you know leads to the trackless desert, where you have a 50 percent chance of being eaten by giant sand-worms. You can eliminate (e)—stand there and whimper—for obvious reasons.

Ready? Go. You have 10 seconds to decide what to do. If you choose wrong, it's going to be very painful. Meanwhile, your fight-or-flight enzymes are pulsing through your veins, and it's really not a good time to make nuanced decisions.

It would have been nice to have memorized and practiced a *simple*, easy-to-remember approach to situations like this. Why simple? Well— imagine that you have worked out a *complex* algorithm that helps you solve "running from space pirate with light saber" situations. You know you figured it out . . . you use an equally complex mnemonic to help you remember it. But it's hard to bring to mind because you're running for your life. If you only slowed down, you could pin it down . . . no, no! The guy's right behind you! Oh, whatever. Just go straight ahead into the alley. Which is a dead end. Me Boba, you grapefruit. So much for the complex approach.

In case you're thinking that *you'd* never run down that blind alley, just remember that it's hard to make complex decisions under stress. Having a simple system not only makes your decisions easier, but it also reduces overall stress by giving you a mental habit to fall back on.

We hope you will never have to practice for a "running from a space pirate" exam. But we *know* you will have to practice for a multiple-choice exam. So, here's The Approach.

The Approach

1. <u>Scan</u> the call of the question and the answer choices.

2. <u>Read</u> the fact pattern and mark legal issues, facts, and categories.

3. <u>Read</u> the call of the question and the answers.

4. <u>Answer</u> the question.

5. Finish the test and <u>then</u> review.

CHAPTER 9

Scanning the Call of the Question and the Answer Choices

Step 1: Before you read the fact pattern, scan the call of the question[12] and answer choices to look for legal terms that give you clues to what issues or causes of action the fact pattern will raise.

Scan, don't *read*

In this chapter, we focus on scanning (not reading) both the call of the question and the answer choices first. Beware! This step may go against the advice of your doctrinal professors. Many professors tell their students, "Don't read the answers first. Read the fact pattern carefully before you look at any answers."

While this advice is well meant, we think it's misleading. It's true—you shouldn't read the answers before reading the fact pattern. But the key

---

12. The "call of the question" consists of one or more sentences, usually at the end of a multiple-choice fact pattern, that tell you what the multiple-choice question is really about. The call of the question is often in the form of a query. Operatively, it usually limits the scope of the question to a particular topic or sub-topic. For example, on the Multistate Bar Exam, the call of the question might be, "Assuming Magda is a law enforcement officer, in which parts of Jun's space is she allowed to search?" This call of the question would tell you that the subject matter of the question is criminal procedure. On the other hand, let's say the call of the question is, "Assuming Jun is Magda's tenant, what causes of action does she have against him?" This tells you the question is a property question. Almost all multiple-choice questions have a "call of the question" component.

term here is *read*. When you read answer choices, bad things happen. So there are two things you shouldn't do.

Multiple-Choice Don'ts

1. Don't *read* the call of the question and answers first. (*Scan* them instead.)
2. Don't read *or* scan the fact pattern first in the call of the question. (Scan the *answers*.)

Why do bad things happen when you read rather than scan? For the same reason you're having problems with multiple choice in the first place. Multiple-choice questions are *too fast*. Most of you can handle issue spotting and analysis when you face it during the hour or more it takes to answer an essay question. Writing clarifies your thoughts, cleans out the mistaken assumptions you made during your initial reading of the question, and often brings up important issues you missed the first time around.

In contrast, during the two minutes (or less) you have to read and answer a multiple-choice question, you revert to instinct. Instinct tells you to do foolish things that probably worked once before but are almost certainly not going to work this time around. Here are a few examples of instinctive decision making.

- **Choosing the answer that sounds like something the professor said in class.** This is a fairly common mistake. It's hard to think when you're reading a multiple-choice question. When you're not thinking, your brain goes into recognition mode. Your brain: "Wait! Stop! '*Danger invites rescue!*' Professor X said that in class five or six times! That must be the right answer!" Even after you read the question, you may be so attached to this answer that you find ways to make the question fit what you've already decided is the right answer. On the other hand, you may read the question and notice that it deals with a business tort. Oops, no rescue there. In that case, it takes time to extricate yourself from your preconception about the question and reconfigure your understanding.

- **Choosing the answer that has a correct statement of the law.** This is a typical red herring. Professors know you're looking for shortcuts, and they discourage prereading by including answers like "Admissible because hearsay does not apply to statements not offered to prove the truth of the matter asserted." If you had read the question, however, you would have seen that it deals with the best evidence rule. Ouch.

- **Choosing the most detailed answer.** Professors are lazy—everybody knows that. If they were hard-working, they would still be practicing law. Therefore, they wouldn't spill a lot of ink in writing a long, detailed answer if it wasn't the right one. Right? No, wrong. Brain overload bonus: *two* detailed answers! One of them must be right! Right? Wrong. Professors can write very long answers that say absolutely nothing, just to mess with your head.

- **Choosing the answer that is different from all the others.** Clever students "realize" that professors include three misleading answers in one area of doctrine to weed out all the students who don't realize that the *real* answer is the one that is different from all the others! Bad move, clever students. This pattern is just commonplace enough to completely screw over those who use it as a choosing method.

- **Choosing the answer that "feels right."** This is the catchall for all of the above categories and explains why professors will tell you not to read the questions. Reading the questions gives you a pre-rational attachment to certain answers. Worse still, you have invested time reading the fact pattern carefully, which discourages you from rereading it and losing time. So when you look at the answers, you're short on time, you're nervous, and you don't want to reread the question. These conditions create a situation ripe for bad decision making. "Okay, okay, okay . . . that one! Whatever! Oh my god, look at the time!"

Okay, you (and your professor) think—"but then I should read the fact pattern first. Then I can form a tentative conclusion about the issues, and it'll be way easier to choose the right answer." Okay, look at the following question and figure out the issues.

Mac is a licensed building contractor. Janet is a house flipper—she buys houses, remodels them, and resells at a higher price (she hopes). Mac has remodeled three or four houses for Janet.

On October 10, Janet sent Mac a fax on her letterhead that simply read: "Mac: Can you remodel the Collier mansion? I'll give you $70K if you provide materials. Connemara marble floor tiles are of the essence." Mac e-mailed Janet the next day. "Can't start until next year at this time. No Connemara marble available till then." He pressed Send but didn't notice that the e-mail got stuck in his outbox and was never sent. Janet didn't hear from Mac, so she called and left a message on Mac's cell phone, saying, "So, you're too big to return my calls. Well, there're lots of other contractors in town." Mac got the message. He responded with an obscene text message from his cell phone.

On October 12, Mac was offered several tons of Connemara marble at bargain prices. He e-mailed Janet again. The e-mail read, "You've got a deal on the Collier mansion. I don't want any money; I want to have the option to buy the mansion for a firm price of $750K." He pressed Send, and at the same time, the earlier e-mail that had been stuck in his outbox was also sent. They appeared in Janet's inbox, right next to each other. Janet was confused and annoyed, and still angry about the rude text message. Later that same day, she called and left another message for Mac, saying, "I'm hiring another contractor." This statement was not true.

Okay, you think—this is easy. This question involves a classic contracts "mailbox rule" offer and acceptance issue, with an electronic twist. Difficult, but you know what it's about. "Offers are valid when transmitted, revocations when . . ." Now, here's the call of the question, followed by the answer choices.

Assume that, absent affirmative defenses, there is a contract between Mac and Janet. The best affirmative defense Janet can raise to prevent enforcement of the contract is

a. the Statute of Frauds, because the subject of the contract is real property.
b. mutual mistake, because Janet was confused by Mac's two e-mails and Mac didn't know his first e-mail wasn't sent until he sent the second one.
c. the Statute of Frauds, because the Collier mansion could not be remodeled in less than a year.
d. none; there are no valid affirmative defenses.

If you had scanned the call of the question and answer choices first, you never would have touched on the mailbox rule—though you *would* have had to figure out which was the valid offer and which was the valid acceptance. But instead of misconstruing the issue and analyzing whether Janet had revoked the offer before Mac's acceptance was valid, you would have realized that you could leap over all that. Scanning the call of the question and answer choices would have told you that this question is about affirmative defenses, not the mailbox rule.

Habit is the enemy of reason—but it doesn't need to be

In law school, quickly scanning the call of the question and answer choices will enable you to determine the issues being tested before reading the facts. This will enable you to then read the fact pattern efficiently looking *only* for the issues or causes of actions found in the answer choices.

On the bar exam, quickly scanning the call of the question and answer choices will enable you to determine the area of law *and* the issues being tested before reading the fact pattern. This is especially important when dealing with the Multistate Bar Exam (MBE) because the MBE tests eight areas of law[13] in 200 questions. The questions do not identify the area of law that is being tested, nor are the questions segregated by area. The examinee must determine which area of law is being tested on a question-by-question basis.

Now scanning is not easy, especially at first. You will be constantly tempted to start by reading the fact pattern or even by slowly and carefully reading the call of the question and answer choices. It's perfectly natural—you want to be *certain*, and the sooner the better. Ward off that certainty, just long enough to scan the answer choices and narrow your field of inquiry.

Eventually, when scanning becomes part of your system, it will become a *habit*—but instead of being a bad habit, it will be a habit that frees up more of your mind for reasoning.

Here's an example of a call of the question and answer choices.

If Tom killed Jerry because of the threat to his own life, Tom should be found

a. not guilty, because of the defense of duress.
b. not guilty, because of the defense of necessity.
c. guilty of first-degree murder.
d. guilty of second-degree murder.

By quickly scanning the question and answer choices looking for legal terms and terms that narrow legal issues, you should see this:

---

13. The eight MBE subjects are civil procedure, constitutional law, contracts, criminal law, criminal procedure, evidence, property, and torts.

** *** ****** ***** ******* ** *** ****** ** *** *** ****, *** ****** ** *****

a. *** ******, ******* ** *** defense of duress.
b. *** ******, ******* ** *** defense of necessity.
c. ****** ** first-degree murder.
d. ****** ** second-degree murder.

Now you can read the fact pattern knowing that the topic of the question is criminal law—homicide (first- and second-degree murder) and the defenses of duress and necessity.

Here's another example.

Reilly's testimony is

a. admissible as a present sense impression.
b. admissible to impeach Max.
c. inadmissible, because Peter may not impeach his own witness.
d. inadmissible, because it is hearsay not within any exception.

By quickly scanning the question and answer choices looking for legal terms, you should see this:

****** ********** **

a. ********** ** * present sense impression.
b. ********** ** impeach ***.
c. ***********, ****** ***** *** *** impeach his own witness.
d. ***********, ******* ** ** hearsay not within any exception.

Now you can read the fact pattern knowing that the topic of the question is evidence—hearsay, nonhearsay, and impeachment.

Notice that you are looking for *legal terms* and *legal categories*—not factual categories. Don't let long answers confuse you. Do keep your mind open, in case the answer choices include several areas of law. That's okay—knowing that your answer choices are limited to certain property torts (conversion, trespass, trespass to chattels) is a lot better than knowing the question is just about torts.

CHAPTER 10

Reading the Fact Pattern

*Step 2: After you scan the call of the question and answer choices, **read the fact pattern.** Mark it up as you would an essay question. Actively read for facts relating to the issues, sub-issues, or causes of actions raised in the answer choices.*

Now, after scanning the call of the question and answer choices, you're finally allowed to do what you've been wanting to do all along: *Read* the fact pattern! But before you start, let's review what you know at the end of Step 1:

- If you are a law student, you now know which area or areas of your subject are covered in this question. For example, you now know that the question deals with adverse possession or easements.

- If you are taking the MBE, you also have figured out that it's a property question.

- If you are a law student and haven't figured out you're sitting in a property exam, you need *a lot* more sleep.

Reading a multiple-choice fact pattern is not like reading a newspaper article. With the knowledge you now have, your reading needs to be *directed.* Once again (here we go), you need a system for spotting and doing a preliminary evaluation of the issues.

Spotting issues is a mysterious procedure (hence the quotation from Einstein that appears at the beginning of Part Two). Although we can talk around it, the mental process that goes into spotting, evaluating, narrowing, and resolving the sub-issues in a fact pattern will be personal to you. But it might go something like this.

1. Scan the call of the question.

> ******** **** ***** ** no issue of consent, ******* **** ***** ** *****
> ******* ***** **

From scanning the call of the question, I know that this question does *not* concern the issue of consent. I don't know what the issue is yet, but I suspect it's an intentional tort.

2. Scan the answers.

> ******** ***** ** no issue of consent, ******* **** ***** ** ***** *******
> ***** **
>
> a. assault, ******* ***** *** ** imminent apprehension of an offensive touching.
> b. battery, ******* ***** ********* ** offensive touching ** *****.
> c. both a and b.
> d. neither a nor b ******* ***** did not have malicious intent.

From scanning the answers, I know that the fact pattern will deal with whether the plaintiff was actually in imminent apprehension of a harmful or offensive touching, or whether the harmful or offensive touching of battery requirement has been met. Now I understand why consent could have been an issue, but has been excluded. I also know that no issue of intent is involved. Finally, because the answer choices include the words *battery* and *assault*, I know that I will have to mentally test each element of each tort.

You can also read the answers even more simply—it's faster, and if you take a while to read the fact pattern, those few seconds may be precious. Here's a simpler scan.

******** ***** ** no issue of consent, ******* **** ***** ** ***** *******
***** **

a. assault ******* ***** *** ** ******** ************ ** ** ********
   ********.
b. battery ******* ***** ****** ** ********* ********** *****.
c. both a and b.
d. neither a nor b ******* ***** *** *** **** ********* ******.

WE ARE NOW AT THE END OF STEP 1 OF THE APPROACH

Now it's time to read the fact pattern (Step 2). The following represents the thought process you *might* go through while reading the fact pattern.

Davey, a 10-year-old boy, jerked the merry-go-round at the playground when eleven-year-old Patty was standing on it. Patty fell off the merry-go-round and hit her head, injuring herself. Immediately before he jerked the merry-go-round, Davey put his hands on the merry-go-round's push bar and said, "I'm going to do it!" Patty said, "Do what?"

3. I mentally exclude the defense or issue of *consent*, and I assume that this would also eliminate any *implied license* or *implied consent* issues that arise from the action taking place on a playground.

4. Okay, now I'm going to look at *assault*, which occurs when the defendant acts, intending to produce an offensive touching or

imminent apprehension thereof, and the plaintiff is in fact placed in imminent apprehension thereof. No touching has to occur.

5. Looking at the facts, I see that Davey and Patty had a verbal exchange. Davey says, "I'm going to do it!" and Patty says, "Do what?" I know from my studies that the defendant's words are usually good evidence of intent. Here, Davey is very helpful: He says, "I'm going to do it!" But what about Patty's response: "Do what?"

6. I think: To satisfy the element that the plaintiff actually *be* in imminent apprehension of a touching, the plaintiff must reasonably expect the defendant to commit an offensive touching against her. I also know that the plaintiff's expectation is not the same thing as the defendant's intent. In other words, the defendant can *do* something that is designed to produce imminent apprehension in the plaintiff, but if the *act* doesn't achieve its objective—"scaring" the plaintiff, for lack of any better term—there's no actual apprehension.

7. I *may* think of the case *Tuberville v. Savage,* where Tuberville placed his hand on his sword hilt and said to Savage, "If it were not assize-time, I would not take such language from you." The court found that Tuberville's threat was *not* imminent because he disclaimed the threat by saying "If . . ." Here, I note that Davey did *not* disclaim his threat. Like Tuberville, he had his hand on the "weapon"—the push bar—but unlike Tuberville, he didn't say, "If you weren't a girl, I would push this merry-go-round." His threat, while not perfectly clear in itself, was clarified by the fact that his hands were on the push bar of the merry-go-round.

8. On the other hand, I also note that Patty didn't seem to understand him when he said, "I'm going to do it!" The fact pattern doesn't say that Patty screamed "Do what???" in abject terror—so although her response might have been a terrified exclamation or a delaying tactic, her most likely reason for saying it was that she really had no idea what Davey was talking about. Therefore, Patty was not *placed* in imminent apprehension of a harmful or offensive touching (assuming that pushing the merry-go-round was a touching)

because, although it's quite possible that Davey sent the message, the message did not reach Patty—at least, not until she felt the merry-go-round begin to move.

9. Note that if this were an essay exam, I might make the merely colorable argument that the moment the merry-go-round moved, Patty was placed in imminent apprehension of a touching—but I would expect this argument to fail because it is most likely that she fell as soon as the merry-go-round moved and had no time to "apprehend" her fall. Because I expect the argument to fail, I raise and dispose of it instantaneously.

10. Therefore, because *one* element of assault is *most likely not satisfied*, I conclude that Patty will not be able to state a case for assault against Davey.

11. Now, while I have been thinking about assault, I have also been thinking about battery—not just because intent is transferable from assault to battery, but also because an actual offensive touching may be evidence of the assault element of imminent apprehension.

12. I know that the elements of battery are: The defendant (1) acts, (2) intending to cause a harmful or offensive touching of the plaintiff, and (3) the harmful or offensive touching does in fact occur (that's my definition, anyway).

13. Okay, I know Davey acted—he pushed the merry-go-round, causing it to jerk. I also know that the push was most likely voluntary and intentional—Davey said, "I'm going to do it!" just before he pushed the push bar. That's enough for intent. Again, although I could argue that his statement is vague, the fact that he pushed the merry-go-round immediately after tells me that his words should be interpreted as, "I'm going to push the merry-go-round."

14. Now I turn to the tougher sub-issue—Davey never actually made contact with Patty. I do know, however, that an *indirect* touching is sufficient for battery. I also remember a case—maybe from the first day of Torts—called *Garrett v. Dailey*, where little Brian Dailey pulled a chair out from under old Ruth Garrett when she was

"engaged in the slow process of sitting down." Brian never *touched* Ruth, but he caused Ruth to touch the ground by exploiting the high probability that she would continue to sit once he had pulled away the chair. This is what the court meant by "knowledge with substantial certainty."

15. Here, Davey saw that Patty was standing on the merry-go-round. Standing, not sitting. If Patty was sitting on the merry-go-round, it would be hard to argue that he knew she would probably fall when he jerked the merry-go-round. But because she was standing, this fact pattern is a lot like *Garrett*—Davey knew something would happen when he jerked the merry-go-round, and it was almost certainly that Patty would stumble or fall. It's not necessary for him to know that she could hit her head, any more than it was necessary for Brian to know Ruth would break her hip when she sat on the ground.

16. Accordingly, I can now conclude that (1) Brian acted, (2) intending to make Patty fall by jerking the merry-go-round, and (3) Patty actually fell, "touching" something hard enough for her to injure her head. Therefore, Patty can state a cause of action for battery against Davey.

WE ARE NOW AT THE END OF STEP 2 OF THE APPROACH

Whew! Would you believe that this entire sequence of thought occurs in two minutes or less? But the apparently meandering sixteen segments of Step 2 actually use a number of the techniques described below.

So if you don't have a system for reading the fact pattern, here are some suggestions.

1. Read actively by asking yourself: Why is this sentence in the fact pattern?

   • That question is *informed* by the fact that you have already scanned the answer choices and you know that this problem deals with assault and/or battery, both of which are intentional torts. You are *looking* for facts that relate to those torts.

- For example, let's ask why this sentence is in the fact pattern: "Immediately before he jerked the merry-go-round, Davey put his hands on the merry-go-round's push bar and said, "'I'm going to do it!'"

    ○ Three things should jump out at you about this sentence: (1) "Immediately before"; (2) "Davey put his hands on the ... push bar," and (3) "[Davey] said, "'I'm going to do it!'"

    ○ *Immediately* is a lot like *imminent*—and imminence is usually an issue in assault.

    ○ The fact that Davey put his hands on the push bar shows that he *acted*—either to place Patty in imminent apprehension of a touching or to actually carry out a touching. You don't have to resolve that yet.

2. Use your pen or pencil and annotate the facts that relate to the issues or causes of actions mentioned in the answer choices. By annotating, we mean circle or underline the facts and write the issue or cause of action the facts relate to in the margin.

    - For example, in reading the Davey and Patty fact pattern, I would be looking (again) for facts relating to intent, voluntary act, or causation. Seeing "jerked the merry-go-round," I would write **act-battery** in the margin, or possibly just **act**.

    - If the issues had *not* been excluded in the call of the question, seeing the word "playground," I might underline it and write **assumption of risk** or **implied license** in the margin.

3. Be wary of unused facts. Read them more than once and consider again whether these facts trigger an issue.

    - If you fail to note anything about Patty saying "Do what?" then you're missing a possible issue about whether Patty actually was in imminent apprehension of a harmful or offensive touching.

4. Circle or underline words in the fact pattern that may have legal consequences. For example, in reading a contracts question, you would want to know whether the agreement was "in writing"

because that fact relates to the Statute of Frauds (an issue you know is important because you saw it in the answer choices).

5. If you are unclear about the issues from the answer choices, read the fact pattern and ask whether any fact or facts in the sentence trigger an issue. If so, circle or underline the fact or facts and identify the issue you believe it triggers.

   • It's easy to miss something, so if something in the fact pattern doesn't make sense, scan the call of the question or the answer choices again. Think about the elements of the legal categories in the answer choices. Then read the sentence that doesn't make sense.

6. **A note about highlighters:** Do *not* use a highlighter to identify key facts. Most professors put facts in an exam for a reason. If you highlight every fact that has meaning for your answer, you will find that almost your entire exam is highlighted, and you won't know why you highlighted anything because you can't make notes with a fat yellow pen with translucent ink. Use a pen or pencil rather than a highlighter. That will help you start organizing the facts while you read.

Let's try again, with a different question.

Putting it together, using the steps

Step 1: No words in the call of the question identify or limit the issues, as in the Davey and Patty example (i.e., "no issue of consent"). So you scan the answer choices and see this.

** * **** ******* *** *** *****, *** ***

a. ******* *** battery ******* ***** ******** ** *** *** **** *** ***** ******.

b. ******* *** assault ******* *** ******** ********** ************ ** ***** *** ** *****.

c. *** ******* *** false imprisonment ******* ***** *** *** ****** ** ******* ***.

d. *** ******* *** intentional infliction of emotional distress ******* *****'* ******* **** ********** ***** *** *************.

From scanning, you know that the area of law is torts—battery, assault, false imprisonment, and intentional infliction of emotional distress.

Step 2: Now read and mark the fact pattern.

Dan, an avid sports fan, was wearing his University of B (U of B) sweatshirt the day after the big cross-town rivalry between U of B and University of C. Dan ran into the U of B's Coach in the men's room of the popular sports bar, Sports Zone. Dan, disgusted with U of B's performance at the big game, said to Coach, "When are you going to learn to coach football? The last three football programs you took over all tanked with you as head coach! U of B should dump you!" As the angry Coach, with clenched fists, advanced on Dan, Dan backed into one of the stalls. Coach shouted, "You think you know about football! You don't know ****! Where's your Heisman trophy? If you weren't a U of B fan, I'd slug you!" Coach turned and started walking away. Just before he left the men's room, he grabbed a handful of dirty towels from the trash and threw them at Dan. One of the towels just missed hitting Dan.

Marking the fact pattern would look something like this:

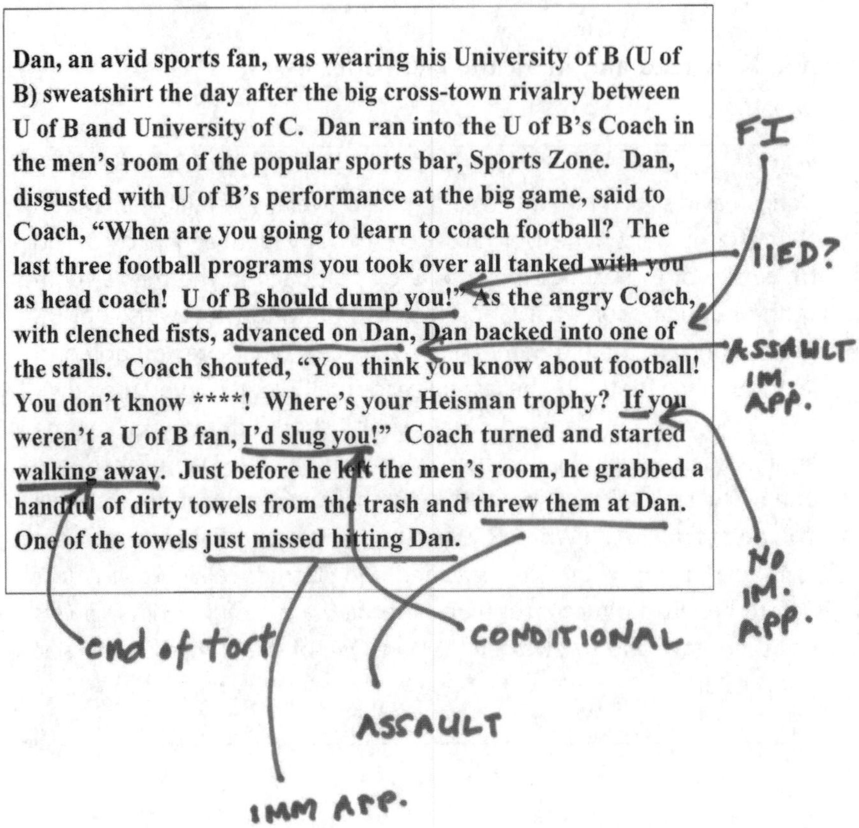

Dan, an avid sports fan, was wearing his University of B (U of B) sweatshirt the day after the big cross-town rivalry between U of B and University of C. Dan ran into the U of B's Coach in the men's room of the popular sports bar, Sports Zone. Dan, disgusted with U of B's performance at the big game, said to Coach, "When are you going to learn to coach football? The last three football programs you took over all tanked with you as head coach! U of B should dump you!" As the angry Coach, with clenched fists, advanced on Dan, Dan backed into one of the stalls. Coach shouted, "You think you know about football! You don't know **! Where's your Heisman trophy? If you weren't a U of B fan, I'd slug you!" Coach turned and started walking away. Just before he left the men's room, he grabbed a handful of dirty towels from the trash and threw them at Dan. One of the towels just missed hitting Dan.**

FI
IIED?
ASSAULT
IM. APP.
NO IM. APP.
CONDITIONAL
end of tort
ASSAULT
IMM APP.

Now if all you were doing was marking the fact pattern, you wouldn't be much of a test taker. You are also *thinking* about the problem and drawing a few tentative conclusions, ruling out some conclusions, and keeping others open until you've read the answer choices.

Here's what you might be thinking as you make these notes:

1. "Dan ... said to Coach, 'When are you going to learn to coach football? The last three football programs you took over all tanked with you as head coach! U of B should dump you!'"

   Intentional infliction of emotional distress? Dan's behavior must be "extreme and outrageous." Well, Dan's words are outrageous—but are they extreme? Does he have a position of power over Coach? Yeah, fans can really wound a coach by saying mean things, but part of being a coach is dealing with annoying, angry fans. Unless Dan backs his words up with fists or physically threatens Coach, I don't think Coach has a cause of action against Dan.[14]

2. "... the angry Coach, with clenched fists, advanced on Dan ..."

Okay, my choices are all intentional torts: assault, battery, false imprisonment, and intentional infliction of emotional distress. No contact, no battery yet. Clenched fists—is that enough for assault? Would a reasonable person think contact is imminent when Coach is not actually winding up for a punch? Probably not. But the word "angry"—some evidence of intent, if something else happens, especially since he "advanced" on Dan.

3. "... Dan backed into one of the stalls."

Why? Retreat—wait a minute, there's no discussion of self-defense, Coach isn't suing Dan. He's in a stall—wait a minute, an enclosed space! False imprisonment. Actually confined? Yes. Did Coach intend to confine him? Well, he didn't push him into the stall—Dan retreated. How long? Oh yeah, look—Coach spoke and then walked away. I think you have to be confined for more than an instant. Also, intent to confine is sketchy. False imprisonment looks like a bad bet.

4. Okay, how about Coach's words? "'You think you know about football! You don't know ****! Where's your Heisman trophy? If you weren't a U of B fan, I'd slug you!'"

These are nasty words, but come on—it's a men's room in a bar, the two guys are talking sports, and there's no special relationship that would make Coach's words especially wounding. The defendant's words need to be extreme and outrageous.

---

14. The Approach doesn't prohibit you from picking up a few words in the call of the question—which would tell you that your answer choices are narrowed to causes of action initiated by Dan against Coach. For the purposes of this illustration, however, we assume that you scanned the answer choices, did not focus too much on the call of the question, and are still keeping in play the possibility that Coach could sue Dan.

Intentional infliction of emotional distress looks like a bad bet on this action, unless Coach does something else.

5. Assault? "If you weren't a U of B fan, I'd slug you!"

    Looking at Coach's words makes me think of the classic disclaimer of what does *not* constitute assault. It's like that case where the dude says, "If it were not assize time, I would not take such language from you."[15] What's assize time? Need to look it up. Why didn't the prof say anything? Maybe he did, it was the first day of class. Hey, *focus*! But Coach says, "If you weren't a U of B fan," and Dan is wearing a U of B sweatshirt, so his *words* aren't assault, but taken together with his advancing on Dan, maybe a reasonable person would think he was in imminent danger of getting slugged.

6. Then "Coach turned and started walking away."

    Huh. Well, that lets out battery. I thought Coach was going to hit him. And no intentional infliction of emotional distress, and bad facts for false imprisonment. I'm screwed—no intentional torts!

7. Wait! The towels! Coach "grabbed a handful of dirty towels from the trash and *threw them* at Dan. One of the towels *just missed hitting* Dan."

    Did he intend? Yes! He threw the towels at Dan—either intended to hit him (dirty paper towels are hard to control) or intended to scare him because who wants to be hit with dirty paper towels? Voluntary action? Yup, threw them. Was Dan in imminent apprehension of being touched? Oh, yeah. I would be. Well, let's say maybe, but I'm scraping the bottom of the barrel now and I need to pick one of the answers. Best bet seems to be assault for the paper towels.

So, this may be your thoughts—disorganized, frantic, but reasonably coherent. Not organized, however. What is organized? The *notes* in the margin are organized. Each one of them represents your thoughts. Reviewing them, you will be able to call up the rule and application when evaluating the answer choices.

---

15. *Tuberville v. Savage, see supra.* Yes, it's one of our favorite cases.

Writing the notes themselves also helps you *think*—the notes cement the legal categories in your mind and make them real. Without the notes, ideas are just floating around in your brain, unmoored to any facts. So get that pen or pencil out (*not* a highlighter) and *mark up* the fact pattern.

Having marked the fact pattern, you are now ready to *read* the call of the question and the answers, which is the subject of the next chapter.

Choosing the Answer

Okay, up to now . . .

1. You have *scanned* (not read) the call of the question and answer choices to narrow the issues. While you did this, of course, you also did a certain amount of thinking about the elements or factors that correspond to the legal categories (or issues) in the answer choices.

2. You have *read* the fact pattern and marked what you think are the issues—again, keeping in mind the elements or factors that correspond to those issues. You have also reached some tentative conclusions about what might be the resolution of those issues.

   You are also aware that the resolution of those issues is not simply a function of whatever you can argue (as it would be in an essay exam). You're limited by the answer choices—not just the possible legal categories (acceptance, not offer; venue, not joinder) but also, very likely, the reasons that you are allowed to use in reaching a conclusion.

You're not done with your pen or pencil, so don't put it down. You will now be reading the call of the question and answer choices with the same laser-like focus and mental agility that you brought to the fact pattern itself, and now you will be drawing *final* conclusions—so you *really* don't want to be doing this all in your head. Using a pen or pencil will allow you to eliminate answer choices clearly and categorically, leaving your mind clear to consider only the answer choices that are left over.

First, a few tips on reading the answer choices.

1. Circle key words that indicate *conditions*.

   - Look for words like *if, only if, unless, not, must, may*.

   - These words can show up anywhere but usually show up in the answer choices, not the call of the question.

2. Look for words that *narrow your choices*.

   - Look for words like *because, best answer, worst answer, most likely, least likely*.

   - These words can also show up anywhere, but are more likely to show up in the call of the question because it *narrows your choice* for all of the answer choices.

3. Eliminate *obvious* wrong answers. An answer is obviously wrong if it

   - incorrectly states the facts, or

   - incorrectly states the law.

   Hint: One way to eliminate wrong answers is to mark each answer as **true** or **false**. Eliminate all false answers by writing a *big* **F** next to the answer choice.

It's the moment you've been waiting for! You finally get to *read* the answer choices. Take exactly *one second* to pat yourself on the back for displaying superhuman self-control and perseverance.

In a suit between Dan and Coach, Dan will

a. prevail for battery, because Coach intended to hit Dan with the dirty towels.
b. prevail for assault, because Dan suffered reasonable apprehension of being hit by Coach.
c. not prevail for false imprisonment, because Coach did not intend to confine Dan.
d. not prevail for intentional infliction of emotional distress, because Coach's actions were reasonable under the circumstances.

Now go ahead and mark up the answer choices. For this question, also write down the reasons for your decisions in the space provided below. (We wouldn't expect you to include this step on the actual test.)

a. _____
   _____(T/F)_____

b. _____
   _____(T/F)_____

c. _____
   _____(T/F)_____

d. _____
   _____(T/F)_____

Now let's review your choosing process. Here is what you may have been thinking.

1. Oh boy, not good. Suit between Dan and Coach? You mean it can go either way? No, wait a minute. The call of the question *narrows* the choices because it says, "Dan will" and there are no defenses, so Dan is the plaintiff, despite his name beginning with "D" (like "defendant"), which is the unimaginative professor's substitute for thinking of party names. So Dan is suing Coach.

2. Okay, (a)—"Prevail for battery because Coach intended to hit Dan with the dirty towels." Something seems wrong about this answer because intent to cause contact is necessary but not sufficient to prove battery. Now I know that Coach did not actually hit Dan with the dirty towels, so I can eliminate this answer. So this answer is not about intent, but about contact. Typical professorial gambit— pretending to talk about one thing and really talking about another. Not true. Mark **F**.

3. Let's look at (b). "Prevail for assault because Dan suffered reasonable apprehension of being hit by Coach." Wait a minute—that's not the rule for assault! It has to be *imminent* apprehension. Okay, let's assume it's a correct rule statement. Was it reasonable for Dan to think he would be hit by Coach? No, probably not. And this isn't about the towels, it's about getting "hit"—with

fists, I guess because it doesn't mention towels. And Coach said, "If you weren't a U of B fan . . . ," so it's *not* reasonable. Mark **F**.

4. Two down, two to go. And it has to be one of these two. Let's read (c). "Not prevail for false imprisonment because Coach did not intend to confine Dan." Well, I thought that evidence of intent to confine was pretty sketchy. But you could also argue that if you clench your fists and advance on someone, you've intended to make that person back up, and that's enough *intent* for assault, and intent is transferable from one tort to another. So, it's not a great argument, but it's enough to make me worry about my answer. Still, I've eliminated (a) and (b), and all that's left is (d). This is a "maybe," but a pretty strong "maybe."

5. Last answer: (d). "Not prevail for intentional infliction of emotional distress because Coach's actions were reasonable under the circumstances." What? Were Coach's actions "reasonable"? He yelled at Dan and backed him into a stall! Okay, maybe that's not extreme and outrageous, but calling it "reasonable" is a stretch. So although the conclusion—"not prevail for intentional infliction of emotional distress" is probably correct, the reason is not correct. It's an okay answer, but not as good as (c). But I'm not completely sure. I'm going to write **M** for "maybe" next to (d) and circle (c) because (d) is a weak "maybe" and (c) is a strong "maybe." Right?

Which brings us to a familiar situation: You're pretty sure of (c), but it *could* be (d), and you're running out of time and it doesn't make sense to sit on this question when you have 30 more to answer.

If you have more than one possible answer:

- Make an educated guess and mark the question number by circling it on the test (not the Scantron).

   ○ Circling the number distinguishes the questions where you are guessing at your answers from questions where you are sure of your answer.

- If you have time to review your answers after you finish with the exam, go back and review *only* the answers to the circled question numbers.

- **Important:** Do not go back and review the answers to *all* the questions. Remember, you will not have time to carefully consider all your answer choices again. In your haste, you may change a carefully considered correct answer choice to a wrong one. Review only those questions where you were unsure of your answer.

When reviewing the circled question numbers:

1. Reread the *entire* question as if you are reading it for the first time. That means

   - scan the answer choices,

   - actively read and mark the fact pattern,

   - eliminate the wrong answers and make an educated guess.

     ○ If you have already eliminated certain answers because they contain obviously false statements of law ("Prevail on an action for adverse possession because Pete is a bona fide purchaser for value (BFP)"), don't review those answers again. *But* if the answer depends on reading the fact pattern, then that answer should be in play again. If making that kind of decision is too difficult in the middle of a stressful exam, just do the entire process again.

   Hint: Use another color pen or pencil to help you distinguish the second read from the first read. That way, you can compare your subsequent impressions of the fact pattern with your initial ones and see where you might have gone wrong or changed your mind.

2. Look at your answer. If your subsequent answer choice is the *same* as your earlier answer choice, stick with your answer.

3. If your subsequent answer choice is *different* from your earlier answer choice, mark the question number again by using *another* shape—a square or a diamond, say—to distinguish that answer.

Then change your answer on the Scantron *and*, if time permits, repeat the process a third time. Keep in mind that this will take more time. If you have a lot of questionable answers, consider adjusting your time management strategy during the exam to give you more time to think and answer the questions on the first pass through the exam.

One more time from the beginning...

Let's go back to Patty and Davey and the merry-go-round. Once again, you have scanned the call of the question and the answer choices.

******** ***** ** no issue of consent, ******* **** ***** ** ***** *******
***** **

a. assault, ******* ***** *** ** ******** ************ ** ** ********
********.
b. battery, ******* ***** ****** ** ********* ********** *****.
c. both a and b.
d. neither a nor b ******* ***** *** *** **** ********* ******.

So it's an assault or battery question, and there's no issue of consent.

Here's the fact pattern again. Read it and *mark up* the issues.

Davey, a ten-year-old boy, jerked the merry-go-round at the playground when eleven-year-old Patty was standing on it. Patty fell off the merry-go-round and hit her head, injuring herself. Immediately before he jerked the merry-go-round, Davey put his hands on the merry-go-round's push bar and said, "I'm going to do it!" Patty said, "Do what?"

Now read the call of the question and the answer choices in full.

Assuming there is *no* issue of consent, Patty's *best* cause of action against Davey is

a. assault, because there was an imminent apprehension of an offensive touching.
b. battery, because Davey did commit an offensive touching of Patty.
c. both (a) and (b).
d. neither (a) nor (b), because Davey did not have malicious intent.

Now eliminate certain choices by

- observing language that *limits* your choices, and

- marking choices that contain obviously false statements of fact or law.

a. _____
_____(T/F)_____

b. _____
_____(T/F)_____

c. _____
_____(T/F)_____

d. _____
_____(T/F)_____

Did you get it right? Turn the page to find out.

Answer (and Explanation)

Look for language that narrows your choices.

- As we mention earlier, if you were reading this fact pattern cold, you would have noticed that the action was taking place on a playground, and you might think that Patty had implicitly consented to a touching, or the apprehension of a touching, merely by standing on the merry-go-round (the *implied license* of the playground). But if you read the call of the question, the issue of consent has been eliminated for you.

- Are the ages of the parties important? Well, one of the things you have learned in Torts is that small children, although they are held to a different standard for negligence, are perfectly capable of committing intentional torts: witness four-year-old Brian Dailey in *Garrett v. Dailey*. So let's just go to the answer choices.

- You can eliminate (d) almost immediately. "Malicious intent" is not required for an intentional tort. Put a big "F" next to it.

- Choice (a) is most likely a "no." Imminent apprehension of a touching is like pitch and catch: The defendant must *intend* that the plaintiff be in imminent apprehension (or intend to commit an offensive touching) *and* the plaintiff must *actually* apprehend the imminent touching. It's not a reasonable person standard. Patty's "Do what?" is most likely a remark that indicates incomprehension—not apprehension.

- Because you have eliminated (a), you can also eliminate (c), which is "both (a) and (b)."

- Now, by process of elimination, you have (b). But just to walk through it—Davey committed an indirect touching of Patty (a la *Garrett v. Dailey*) by pushing the push bar and jerking the merry-go-round. His action almost certainly caused Patty to lose her balance, fall, and hit her head. Davey signaled his intent to perform the action—jerking the merry-go-round—by saying "I'm going to do it!" just before he jerked the merry-go-round. Accordingly, Patty's *best* cause of action against Davey is for battery.

You may be asking yourself right now, "How on earth do I do all this in less than two minutes?" Well, you don't. Much of what is written down in detail above takes place in flashes and snap decisions—snap decisions that are accurate and comprehensive because you have practiced The Approach dozens and dozens of times, on different multiple-choice questions in different subjects.

Start out slowly using practice multiple-choice questions. Ideally, the questions should come with answers and explanations. Take as much time as you need. Your first instinct will be to revert to an old habit—reading the fact pattern first, without narrowing the issues; or reading the answer choices and forming early (and often inaccurate) impressions of the issues in the fact pattern. So when we say "slowly," we mean *work* slowly, taking note of what you are doing. Be disciplined about (1) scanning the call of the question and answer choices, then (2) reading and marking up the fact pattern, then (3) reading the call of the question and answer choices, and (4) choosing your answer. (5) Circle any questions whose answers you are uncertain about and, after you have completed the entire exam, go through the entire process again only for those questions.

If you practice The Approach a number of times, you'll find that it's probably more effective than the system you are using. This may not be clear at first, just as it's not immediately clear why you have to brief cases rather than simply make notes in the margin. For that reason, give The Approach some time, before you throw this book across the room and shout, "My old system may not have given me good grades, but at least it was user-friendly!" This system is also user-friendly, but the user needs to do some work first.

But I'm still getting some questions wrong...

No system is perfect—and no user is perfect either. You can confidently expect *not* to achieve perfect scores in future multiple-choice exams. But you can still improve those scores. Using The Approach will improve your score and make you more confident about taking multiple-choice exams. But you still need to master certain skills; learn rules and factors; and practice reading, analyzing, and choosing answer choices.

If you aren't happy with your multiple-choice score, having a system will help—but there's probably something else that you need to improve as well. "I need to study harder" is an admirable sentiment, but "study harder" how? That's what the next part—Part Three, "Evaluating Performance and Diagnosing Problems"—is about. It allows you to target problem areas and improve them, while leaving your strengths untouched.

Like using The Approach, evaluating your own performance and diagnosing your problems can be difficult and time-consuming. In fact, it is the most detailed and labor-intensive part of the process. It also produces surprisingly effective results. Students who have used these techniques have been amazed to find areas of weakness—or areas of competence—that they didn't know they had. Naturally, this occurred after several days or even weeks of wailing and gnashing of teeth, as they carefully annotated their outlines, applied their skills, and tested those skills in practice multiple-choice tests. But the work produced results—so steel yourself, and let's do some self-evaluation.

A Systematic Approach to Improving Multiple-Choice Performance

Part One
TIME MANAGEMENT
Evaluate how you spend your time before the test (preparation) and during the test.

Part Two
THE APPROACH
Create an exam strategy for choosing the right answer.

Practice Multiple-Choice Questions

Part Three
EVALUATING PERFORMANCE AND DIAGNOSING PROBLEMS
Make necessary changes to how you read the questions and/or learn the substantive material.

THE TEST

EVALUATING PERFORMANCE AND DIAGNOSING PROBLEMS

Overview

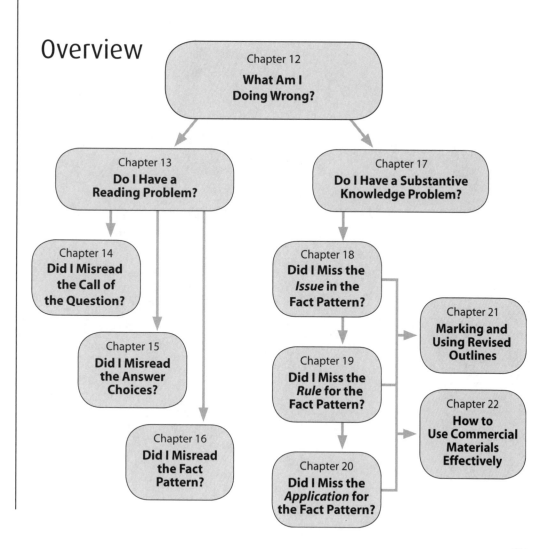

CHAPTER 12

What Am I Doing Wrong?

"The successful man will profit from his mistakes and try again in a different way."

—Dale Carnegie

By now you should have taken at least one practice test using The Approach, and it's time to see how you did. If you answered the vast majority of the questions correctly, congratulations! You don't need to read any further. But if you're not happy with your score, this is the section of the book where we help you identify what you need to do to improve.

To improve your performance on a multiple-choice exam, it is not enough to simply review the answers to the questions you missed and then take another test. You need to identify (1) why you're not getting the correct answers, and (2) how you can correct those weaknesses. Practice, by taking hundreds of multiple-choice questions, won't make perfect if you don't understand what you are doing wrong and what you need to do to fix it.[16]

Identifying and correcting the causes of your exam-taking weaknesses are the most important and the most time-consuming parts of this process. Using the systems described in this section will help you become your own coach so that you can improve your performance. Just as sprinters must watch videos of their races to determine whether their time was slow

---

16. Although some of your professors may suggest answering hundreds of multiple-choice questions to improve your score, in our opinion it is a waste of time and effort to do so without analyzing where you are going wrong.

because they were late off the starting block or because their stride was inefficient, you need to figure out whether

1. **You have a reading problem** (you are misreading the question so you choose the wrong answer), or

2. **You have a substantive knowledge problem** (your understanding of legal rules and their application is incorrect so you choose the wrong answer).

Every student is different, so your exam-taking problems may stem from a problem with reading, with substantive knowledge, or both. Although at first you may think that you only have a reading problem or that you only have a substantive knowledge problem, we have found these two issues are often interrelated. For example, if your substantive knowledge of torts is shaky, that makes it more likely you will misread a torts question in the first place. As a result, paying careful attention to your reading problems may also uncover the weaknesses in your substantive understanding of the issues and vice versa.

This is why we recommend reading all the chapters in this section even though you may think that they don't all apply to you. In Chapter 13, we explain the kinds of reading problems students have and how to correct them. Chapter 17 addresses how a lack of substantive knowledge affects multiple-choice exam performance and provides steps to diagnose and correct these deficiencies. Then in Chapter 22, we discuss the problems that can arise in using commercial or canned outlines to prepare for a multiple-choice exam.[17]

While all of this may seem overwhelming, breaking up your exam-taking weaknesses into smaller, concrete issues actually makes them easier to correct. Taking the time to figure out the cause of your poor multiple-choice exam taking skills will save you time in the long run; you will be able to correct your mistakes and then *retest only those areas where you miss the correct answers* until you are sure that you have corrected your reading

---

17. In case you think we are skipping chapters, please note: Chapters 14 through 16 cover different types of reading problems, and chapters 18 through 21 discuss types of substantive knowledge deficiencies. Don't skip these chapters.

skills and your substantive knowledge. It is this process of *targeted exam practice* after you diagnose your weaknesses that will help you to master the law school multiple-choice exam.

Getting ready to use part three

Before reading further, gather the following materials so you can figure out which exam-taking problems you are having.

1. **The questions, including explanatory answers, that you missed on your practice test.**

   Before using Part Three, you should have taken one practice multiple-choice exam and identified the questions you got wrong. To identify your particular exam-taking weaknesses, you need at least 10 missed questions so you can see the patterns causing you to miss the correct answer. We recommend at least 10 if the test is a single subject test (i.e., all torts, all contracts, etc.), and at least 20 missed questions if you are practicing the Multistate Bar Exam questions.[18] For all of your missed questions, be sure that you have the fact pattern, answer choices, and explanatory answers.

   If you missed *fewer* than the required number of questions, good job! Now take another test. We hope you continue to score well, but if you start missing more questions, it may mean that you didn't identify a deficient subject area on the first test. Better you know that now than in the middle of an actual exam!

2. **The outlines and study materials that you used to prepare for that test.**

   To help you identify and correct problems in your substantive knowledge, be sure to have on hand any outlines, flash cards, or study aids that you have used, including (1) those that you prepared

---

18. We recommend more missed questions for the MBE to more easily show whether your weakness is primarily in one or two particular subject areas that require further study.

yourself, (2) those you obtained from other students or study groups, and (3) those commercial outlines and study aids that you studied directly or used to help create your own study aids to prepare for that test.

Once you have all these materials together, you are ready to begin diagnosing your exam-taking problems.

CHAPTER 13

Do I Have a Reading Problem?

When professors and bar examiners write multiple-choice questions, they try to write legal questions that have clear "right" answers. This is different from essay exam questions, which usually require students to discuss the *ambiguities* in a legal situation. Because a multiple-choice question has to have a right answer, the exam writers use drafting techniques to make it harder to choose the right answer when you are in a hurry. After all, if the right answers were obvious, everyone would do well. These drafting techniques cause students to choose the wrong answer, *even when they know the correct rule and how to apply it to the facts.*

To determine whether you are missing the correct answer because you have a reading problem, take a look through the fact patterns and questions you got wrong on your practice test and ask yourself the following questions.

- Do I miss questions in many different areas of the subject matter being tested?
- Do I get the correct answer when I am able to read the facts and the questions and answers slowly?

If the answer to one or both of these questions is "yes," then you probably had reading problems when you took the practice test.

For example, if you are taking an MBE practice test and you see that seven out of the ten questions you missed were contracts questions, then you have problems with your substantive knowledge of contracts. If you are taking a property multiple-choice practice exam and you see that five out of ten of the questions you missed are future interest questions, you have a substantive knowledge problem with future interests. But if you see no clear subject area dominating your missed answers, then you are probably misreading the questions.

In addition, if you are able to answer the missed questions correctly when you have more time, this is a strong indicator that your primary issue is a reading problem. Many students find that when they review their incorrect answers, they can't believe they chose the wrong answer because the right answer is so obvious. Such misreading occurs because they have so little time to read and absorb the facts, answers, and calls of the question in the allotted time. Many students rush through and skim facts and questions in an effort to get through the question quickly, but they are thrown off track because they *misread key language.* Misreading key language includes (1) actual misreading (thinking a question asks one thing when it is asking something else), (2) failing to keep the question in mind while reviewing facts and answers, and (3) forgetting the key words when choosing the answer.

DO I HAVE A READING PROBLEM, OR IS IT REALLY A TIME MANAGEMENT PROBLEM?

If your answers to the above questions indicate that you have a reading problem, then the first thing you need to do is to check your time allocations to be sure you are giving yourself enough time to read the questions carefully. By this we mean you should pay attention to your time allocations while you are taking the test. If you followed our instructions in Chapter 6, you should have determined your timing as part of your exam strategy *before* starting the test.

For example, suppose you determined that by question 9 you should be a half hour into the exam. If your exam started at noon, then at question 9 you should be at 12:30 p.m. You mark that time at question 9 before starting the test. After marking your time allocations on the exam, you start taking the exam. When you reach question 9 you see the 12:30 notation. At that point, where are you in your actual timing? Is it only 12:22 p.m.? If your missed answers indicate that you have a reading problem—meaning you misread any part of the questions—then you need to practice slowing down to see if that remedies the problem.

On the other hand, if you are at 12:40 p.m. when you reach question 9 and you have a reading problem, you need to determine whether you are spending too much time on certain questions because you don't know the law[19] (and thus have problems determining which answer to choose) or if you simply need the extra time to read and process the information to select the answer. Note—it could be a little of both.

If the problem is that you spend too much time because you don't know the law, then your problem is likely to be with your time management before the exam—you did not spend enough time studying and learning the material. Remember, learning the material is more than just knowing the black letter law. The correct answer on a multiple-choice exam considers the facts of the precedent cases as well as the policy reasons behind the rule. If you only study the black letter law without studying how that law was applied in the past or the policy reasons behind that law, you miss the subtleties and nuances of the law. This may be why you can only narrow the answer choices down to two rather than one, so you spend unnecessary extra time trying to choose between the two answers.[20]

DO I NEED EXTRA TIME TO COMPLETE THE EXAM?

If the problem is only that you need extra time to read and process the information, then you should do the following.

---

19. This is a substantive knowledge problem.
20. Chapters 17-20 provide a step-by-step breakdown of how to pinpoint and correct the weaknesses in your substantive knowledge.

- Determine how much extra time you need on the exam by moving through a timed practice exam as quickly as you can but still considering each answer choice.

  ○ Note how many questions you completed in the time allocated for the exam. Then finish the exam and note how many more minutes you needed to actually complete the exam.

    For example, suppose the timing for the practice exam is 25 multiple-choice questions in one hour. At one hour, you are at question 23. You finish the exam in one hour, five minutes. You needed only an additional five minutes to complete the exam.

  ○ If you need only a few additional minutes, see if the other suggestions listed below can help you shave off some time and be more effective with your reading.

- If you need more than a few minutes, determine how much extra time you need and then determine whether your need for extra time is consistent in all your classes as opposed to just this one class. For example, do you need more time because you just don't understand property, but you're fine in torts? Or do you need extra time in all your classes?

- Determine whether you need extra time to read and process the information on essay exams as well as multiple-choice exams. And as with multiple-choice exams, determine how much extra time you need on essay exams.

    For example, take a timed practice essay exam. If the time allocated for the essay exam is one hour, work on the essay for an hour. Draw a line on your answer at the end of the hour and then finish the exam. Once you have finished, note how much additional time you needed to finish the exam.

If you find that you need extra time in virtually all your classes, no matter the type of test, then consider consulting with a learning specialist. When consulting with the specialist, relate your exam reading experiences and tell the specialist how much extra time you believe you need for both multiple-choice and essay exams.[21]

WHAT KINDS OF READING ERRORS AM I MAKING?

After you have checked your time allocations, the next step is to determine *how* you are misreading the questions so that you can take steps to avoid those kinds of errors on your next practice test. Did you

- misread the call of the question?

- misread the answer choices?

- misread the fact pattern?

If you are have reading problems while trying to answer complex questions in a brief amount of time, chances are that you are misreading questions, answers, and facts, and not just one or the other of the three. Nonetheless, to identify where you are going wrong in your reading and to figure out how to avoid those mistakes, you want to look at each part of the multiple-choice question separately to see where the bulk of your misreading is occurring. Then you can focus on avoiding those particular reading traps in the future. Accordingly, the next several chapters will address each of these reading errors one at a time.

---

21. In our experience, it is not uncommon for law students to be diagnosed with learning disabilities while in law school. Law school is a unique experience due to the sheer quantity of reading and the need to be precise with facts and rules. If you believe you may have a learning disability, or if you have been told in the past that you may have a disability, get tested and accommodated *while in law school.* Getting a test accommodation for the bar exam is more difficult if you did not have an accommodation while in law school. As for your job after the bar exam, remember you will be in control of the amount of time it takes you to complete a task once you start practicing law.

CHAPTER 14

Did I Misread the Call of the Question?

You cannot select the correct answer on a multiple-choice exam if you don't understand the call of the question no matter how well you know the law.[22] Mistakes in reading the call of the question occur when you read the question too quickly or when you forget the call of the question while reviewing facts and answer choices. When you read the question too quickly, you may think you understand what you are being asked but you are not seeing the key words that indicate what the correct answer is. Often fact patterns will contain red herrings, so if you don't keep the call of the question in mind as you read the facts, you will choose the wrong answer. When reading the call of the question, you want to identify two elements:

1. the topic of law the question is dealing with, and

2. the parameters the question is setting.

IDENTIFYING THE CORRECT TOPIC

First let's look at number one: identifying the correct topic in the call of the question. For example, if you skim the following fact pattern, you would probably expect that this torts question is about false imprisonment.

---

22. Note that sometimes the call of the question is not a full question. In these types of multiple-choice questions, most of the key language indicating what you are being asked to decide may be in the answer choices. In those cases, apply the same suggestions for reading the call of the question to the answers.

> A college student who was merely shopping at the school bookstore was stopped by the store's security guard and taken to the back office, which was a 10 foot square room with no windows. The guard politely told the student, "You match the description of a shoplifter in the area. I'll be right back, I'm going to get the manager. Don't leave." The guard shut the door behind her and locked the door. The student had claustrophobia, and after the guard left, the student suffered a panic attack. When the guard and the manager returned five minutes later, they calmed the student. They discovered that she was not the shoplifter and let her go.

This fact pattern has the following answer choices.

> a. No, because the bookstore confined the student against her will.
> b. No, because the student had no reasonable means of escape.
> c. Yes, because the store had probable cause to detain her and it detained her for a reasonable time and in a reasonable manner.
> d. No, because the student's distress was not severe and the store's conduct was not outrageous.

If you did not read the call of the question carefully, you might select an answer that evaluates whether the required elements of false imprisonment have been satisfied. But look at this call of the question.

> Does the bookstore have a viable defense to the student's false imprisonment claim?
>
> a. No, because the bookstore confined the student against her will.
> b. No, because the student had no reasonable means of escape.
> c. Yes, because the store had probable cause to detain her and it detained her for a reasonable time and in a reasonable manner.
> d. No, because the student's distress was not severe and the store's conduct was not outrageous.

A careful reading of this call of the question tells you to focus on *defenses* to false imprisonment, in this case the merchant's defense to false imprisonment. If you had only skimmed the call of the question, the words "false imprisonment claim" might have jumped out at you and misdirected you to the answers containing the elements of that claim. It is the word "defense" in the call of the question that tells you that the topic of the question is not about false imprisonment, so answers (a) and (b) are wrong because they only address the elements of false imprisonment, not the elements of the defense. Therefore, if you look only at the top three choices, the only one that could be correct is (c) because it is the only answer that includes the elements of the *defense*.

Using The Approach when reading this call of the question, you should have circled the words "viable defense" as well as "false imprisonment." The fact that the call of the question includes a merchant, the bookstore, could also indicate that you should read the fact pattern to see whether the elements of the merchant's defense to false imprisonment have been satisfied.

But sometimes exam writers will be even trickier. What if the call of the question was the following?

Does the student have a viable claim for intentional infliction of emotional distress?

a. No, because the bookstore confined the student against her will.
b. No, because the student had no reasonable means of escape.
c. Yes, because the store had probable cause to detain her and it detained her for a reasonable time and in a reasonable manner.
d. No, because the student's distress was not severe and the store's conduct was not outrageous.

If that were the case, none of the first three answers above could be correct because none of them deal with the tort identified in the call of the question. The only correct answer would be (d) because it is the only answer that identifies elements of intentional infliction of emotional distress.

Here the exam drafters are counting on students not reading carefully enough to notice that the tort is not the one that the beginning of the facts would suggest. It is only in the call of the question that the correct tort is flagged. Thus, when reading this question you would want to have circled "intentional infliction of emotional distress" before you even skimmed through the facts so that you wouldn't have been distracted by the false imprisonment facts.

Another variation on getting the topic wrong occurs when you have the right area of law but the call of the question addresses *only one element* of the claim or doctrine. Thus, the call of the question *narrows* the answer choices. For example, let's assume you have a fact pattern where A has a potential false imprisonment claim against B. The call of the question reads as follows.

> Did B intend to confine A?

The *only* correct answer choices, then, are ones that address the intent-to-confine facts from the fact pattern. Any answer choice that addresses A's opportunity-to-escape facts would be incorrect.

Another way drafters limit the question to one element is to ask you to *assume an element is satisfied* within the call of the question.[23] For instance, here's another way to ask the question above.

> Assuming A was in a locked room and had no opportunity to escape, did B falsely imprison A?

---

23. Or sometimes the drafters will add such assumptions within the answer choices.

Here the dependent clause beginning with the word "assuming" tells you to ignore two of the three required elements for false imprisonment, actual confinement and opportunity to escape. So the only answer choices you should consider are those pertaining to the third requirement, intent to confine. But if you didn't pay attention to the first part of the question and focused only on "did B falsely imprison A?" you might select a wrong answer.

Note for MBE takers

Correctly identifying the topic of a question can be even harder on the MBE because you need to make sure not only that you have identified the correct topics within torts, but also that it is a torts question to begin with. Although many MBE questions state the legal topic outright in the call of the question, many others do not. When exam drafters do not explicitly tell you the topic, you want to look for key words that identify the legal subject immediately to get you on track. For instance, the word "admissible" in the call of the question usually signifies that the MBE question is an evidence question.

In identifying the legal topic of a MBE question, remember that the same kinds of acts may be both a tort and a crime (e.g., battery, assault, killing). Therefore, pay particular attention to the use of the words "liable" and "guilty" in the call of the question. When you see the word "guilty" in the call of the question, you are dealing with criminal law rules, not tort law rules.

In contrast, be very careful when you see words like *reliance* or *foreseeability* in an MBE call of the question. Both torts and contracts use these terms, so one of these words alone will not tell you the legal subject of the question, and they could mislead you into choosing the wrong answer.

These are just a few examples of the ways in which a call of the question on the MBE may give you clues about the legal topic of the question even if the call of the question does not specifically tell you the topic. For MBE takers, note those questions where you answered the wrong topic and try to identify the key language in the call of the question that would have kept you from going off track so that you can avoid these traps on future practice tests.

IDENTIFYING THE PARAMETERS OF THE QUESTION

Now let's look at the second type of misreading problem you might be having when you misread the call of the question: misreading the parameters that the call of the question is setting. With this type of reading problem, you understand what the correct legal topic of the question is, but you are not paying sufficient attention to the *key words that determine what you are being asked to decide about that legal topic.* Is the question asking you to identify whether a particular claim is satisfied by the fact pattern? Is the question asking you about the arguments a party might make to state a claim? Is the question asking you for the factual basis for a potential claim? The key words in the call of the question indicate what kind of analysis you are being asked to do and provide clues as to how you should approach the question. Thus, understanding the call of the question is critical to selecting the correct answer choice.

There can be several kinds of parameters in the call of the question among missed questions:

1. Questions missed because you were *focusing on the wrong actor* when you chose your answer

2. Questions missed because you didn't pay attention to the *point of view* the call of the question was asking you to take

3. Questions missed because *you misread the descriptors* limiting the correct answer

FOCUSING ON THE WRONG ACTOR

Missing a question because you were focusing on the *wrong actor* when you chose your answer is purely an error of reading too quickly and failing to note which character from the fact pattern the question is focusing on.

For example, look at the following question.

> On his lunch break, John was walking by an open window of an archeologist's home when he noticed a gold and ruby bracelet with an unusual design sitting on the desk. John reached inside, grabbed the bracelet, put it in his pocket, and walked away. That evening he gave the bracelet to his girlfriend Maria, telling her that he had bought "this special bracelet for a special girl." Maria was delighted and immediately put the bracelet on. The next day in the local paper, she saw an article in the paper with a picture of the bracelet under the headline "Mayan Treasure Stolen from Archeologist's Home." The article contained a number to call if the reader had any information.
>
> Which of the following best describes the crime Maria has committed?
>
> a. Burglary
> b. Larceny
> c. Receipt of stolen property
> d. None of the above

Here, although *John* may be guilty of burglary or larceny when he took the bracelet from the archeologist's home, the call of the question is asking what crimes *Maria* has committed. She was not the person who took the bracelet or reached into the home, so neither (a) nor (b) applies. Thus your choice should immediately have been narrowed to either (c) or (d).[24] This is a classic misdirect in a call of the question.

---

24. The correct answer here is (d) because Maria had no criminal intent to accept stolen property at the time she took the bracelet.

This kind of misdirect can also occur when the question asks about a generic actor. For instance, the question may ask:

> What is the plaintiff's best argument?

But one or more of the incorrect answers may address the *defendant's* best argument. Don't fall for these false choices.

Another way to misread the call of the question regarding actors or parties occurs when the fact pattern contains *multiple parties with multiples claims or crimes*.[25] For example, look at the following fact pattern and call of the question.

> Abe, Bert, Carlos, and Douggie were members of a crime ring. They all hated Zach, who they believed was going to turn them into the police. Abe and Bert decided to go find Zach and try to kill him. They cornered Zach in an alley, called Zach a rat, and began shoving him backward toward a wall. Just then, Carlos and Douggie showed up. Carlos handed his gun to Abe and told Abe to "finish him off." Bert grabbed Zach, and Abe fired the gun twice at Zach. The first bullet killed Zach instantly. The second bullet hit Carlos, who later died of his wounds at the hospital.
> Is Douggie guilty of murdering Carlos?

Since this fact pattern contains two killings and multiple people are potentially involved, it is crucial to be sure you have noted both the possible murderer and the victim in this call of the question. Each party potentially has a different intent than the others, and each party may have intent to hurt Zach but not Carlos. Therefore the correct answer

---

25. This happens most frequently when several questions are based on a single fact pattern.

depends entirely on *which actor* and *which victim* are named in the call of the question.

If you find that you make this kind of reading error, be sure to mark the actor(s) and any people against whom the action is directed when you are reading the call of the question so you are not distracted by answers that apply to other parties in the fact pattern.

IGNORING THE CALL OF QUESTION'S POINT OF VIEW

Another kind of call of the question favored by exam drafters asks the reader to *apply the point of view of a particular actor in the legal world:* e.g., a judge, a prosecutor or a plaintiff's attorney, a defendant's attorney or a criminal defense attorney, or a law professor.

To illustrate, a question that asks you to stand in the shoes of a judge would be one that begins, "The court should rule in favor of X because . . ." or "Will X prevail?" These kinds of questions are asking you to choose the answer representing the *most likely outcome* if the case went to trial. When standing in a judge's shoes, you may have to consider (1) the claim and its defenses, (2) arguments and counterarguments, and (3) the burden of proof.

In contrast, a question that begins "The prosecutor's best argument is . . ." does not ask you to evaluate which choice is the most likely outcome at trial, it is asking which argument is *both legally accurate and will obtain the best outcome* for the prosecutor. In this situation, you need to keep in mind (1) the party's goal[26] and (2) arguments and counterarguments to achieve that goal.

Consider this example.

---

26. For example, to win at trial, to get evidence admitted, or to collect the highest amount of damages.

Twelve-year-old David was playing tag with his friends when he ran into the street. Just at that moment Shannon, who was driving down the road, looked at her cell phone and failed to see David. Shannon hit David with her car, injuring him. Even though David was hurt, David's father did not take David to the doctor right away because he had an important meeting. As a result, when David finally received treatment, his injuries were more severe than they would have been if he had been treated right away.

What is the *best argument* David's attorney can make to recover damages in a suit against Shannon?

a. David's father's negligence cannot be imputed to his child.
b. David had no duty to seek medical care after an injury.
c. Shannon was negligent when she hit David with her car.
d. The doctrine of avoidable consequences bars recovery only for the aggravation of an injury, not for the original injury.

In this question, while (d) would allow David to recover damages for the original injury, it does not award damages to David for *all* his injuries. David can recover the largest amount of damages if his attorney makes the argument in (a) because (a) is an accurate statement of the law and will obtain the largest amount of damages (the key word in the call of the question). Note that the party's goal (see above) is the key metric for determining what "best" means—not the most complete or coherent argument. The "best argument" here is the one that will produce the best result for David. While answer (c) may be an accurate legal statement about the facts, it is not the *best* argument David's attorney can make. In contrast, when the question asks you to identify the cause of action or claim, the question is asking you to act like a law professor. Your job in these types of questions is to identify which claim or crime's elements are all satisfied by the facts.[27]

---

27. Answer (b) here is an inaccurate statement of the law.

The point to note here: By noting the *point of view* the call of the question is assigning to you, you will not be distracted by answers that are inconsistent with that point of view.

MISREADING DESCRIPTORS THAT LIMIT ANSWER CHOICES

Many multiple-choice questions, such as the example where Shannon hit David with her car, contain *descriptors that determine which answer you are to select.* These include, for example, "the best answer," "the worst answer," "the most likely outcome," and "the least likely outcome."[28] The most obvious misreading mistake students make here is to mix up "best" with "worst" or "most likely" with "least likely." For example, look at the following hypothetical.

> Smith went to a party where he asked the bartender for a nonalcoholic punch. Unbeknowst to Smith, Johnson slipped a strong odorless and tasteless drug into Smith's drink. Smith soon became incoherent and had difficulty walking straight. Smith stumbled toward the dining table, picked up a knife, and began waving it around, yelling, "I won't let you kill me! Stay back, stay back!" Stevens, who was standing nearby talking to another party goer, was slashed in the neck by the knife. Stevens was taken to the hospital, where the doctors said he would recover. Smith has no memory of this incident.
>
> If Smith is charged with assault with a deadly weapon, what is Smith's worst defense?
>
> a. Involuntary intoxication
> b. Voluntary intoxication

---

28. These key words can also be verbs, such as "prevail" or "win" versus "lose."

If you skim this question too quickly, you may be tempted to choose (a) because you know that involuntary intoxication is a good defense to general intent crimes, while voluntary intoxication is not. The exam writers are trying to trick you into choosing the best defense, when in fact the question is asking for the worst one—don't fall for it.

If you find that you missed questions because you selected the *most likely outcome* when the call of the question asked for *the least likely outcome,* then you need to mark those words when you read the call of the question so that you remember what the question is asking when you read through and select the answer.

A trickier version of these kinds of questions asks "Which of the following are true/false?" This phrasing requires you to evaluate several statements before looking at your answer choices. When reading quickly, it is easy to lose track of that fact that you are looking for *all* true or *all* false answers given to the question.

For example, here is a property question.

Adena's grandfather had a painting worth $25,000. At Adena's twenty-first birthday, her grandfather announced that he was giving the painting to Adena for Adena's birthday in front of all of Adena's birthday party guests. Adena's grandfather, who was in excellent health, was hit by a car and passed away a week later. The painting was still hanging in Adena's grandfather's apartment. Adena's grandfather's valid will left "'my entire estate" to Adena's cousin Jesse. The will did not specifically mention the painting.
   Which of the following statements is/are true?

   I. The painting belongs to Adena because Adena's grandfather intended to give the painting to Adena.
   II. The painting belongs to Adena because it was a gift causa mortis.
     a. I only
     b. II only
     c. I and II
     d. Neither I nor II

When you see this kind of call of the question, you should circle the key words "is/are" and "true" to help you keep in mind that you have to evaluate each statement *independently* to determine whether it is true or false. Read statement I and note a **T** or **F** by that statement before you move on to statement II and do the same thing. Only then should you read the answer choices (a), (b), (c), or (d) and chose the right answer depending on whether you see T next to those statements.

Here, you would *not* put a T next to statement I because intent alone is insufficient for a gift (you also need delivery and acceptance). You would *not* put a T next to II because Adena's grandfather did not know he was going to die soon. Seeing no T's next to the two statements, you would chose the correct answer, (d), neither I nor II.

TIME TO EVALUATE

So now turn to the questions that you missed in your practice test. Look at each incorrect answer you selected and then look at the call of the question.

1. **Were you answering the wrong question?**

    That is, did you answer a question about false imprisonment when it should have been an answer about the elements of the defense to false imprisonment? Or were you answering a question about false imprisonment when it was actually a question about the defendant's intent to confine the plaintiff?

    If the answer is "yes," then congratulations! You now understand that you need to pay particular attention to whether you are *identifying the right topic from the call of the question before you ever read the fact pattern.*[29] To do this, spend a little more time when you scan the call of the question. Scan carefully for words that identify the issue and for words that narrow or eliminate issues.

---

29. You should also flag this reading error on your outline. We cover how to do that in Chapter 21.

2. **Was there a pattern in the way the questions were phrased?**

Look for the different kinds of parameters in the call of the question among your missed questions.

a. Did you *focus on the wrong actor* when you chose your answer?

b. Did you miss the *point of view* the call of the question was asking you to take?

c. Did you *misread the descriptors* limiting the correct answer?

If the answer is "yes" to any of these questions, in addition to marking the legal issues, include in your markup the key words that identify the actors, the point of view, and any descriptors that limit the correct answer.

A FINAL NOTE ON MISREADING THE CALL OF THE QUESTION

If you are misreading the call of the question, try to figure out what types of questions are throwing you off and pay special attention to those kinds of questions when you take your next multiple-choice practice test. By focusing on the kinds of questions that throw you, you will become more efficient in correcting your mistakes as you become more comfortable with those particular types of questions.

Practice reading the call of the question to determine what the question is asking you to decide. Keep in mind that some of the same reading issues you may have with the call of the question may be a problem when reading the answer choices, depending on how the question is structured. If, however, you seem to understand the call of the question but are still having reading issues when choosing the correct answer, read the next chapter.

CHAPTER 15

Did I Misread the Answer Choices?

Once you are clear what the call of the question is asking, you want to make sure that you avoid misreading the answer choices, causing you to select the wrong response to the call of the question. For multiple-choice questions on a law school exam, it is usually not enough that you know the correct answer (e.g., "Yes, the plaintiff has a claim" or "No, the defendant cannot be charged with murder"). You must also select *the response with the correct reasoning*, which usually consists of a rule, key facts, or both.[30] Misreading errors occur when selecting an answer choice because

1. you misread the facts in the answer,

2. you misread the legal rule it contained, and/or

3. you did not pay attention to words that indicate conditions or narrow choices.

MISREADING THE FACTS IN THE ANSWER CHOICES

Many answer choices contain reasoning that consists primarily or entirely of facts. When you read such incorrect answer choices too quickly, you

---

30. Note that some simple questions do just ask you to identify the applicable legal claim or theory and nothing more, and consequently you are much less likely to misread these kinds of answer choices.

may fail to notice that the facts included in the answer are wrong. The facts in a wrong answer may *assume facts* that were not in the original fact pattern, or they may *misstate or contradict* the facts included in the fact pattern. Either way, this signals that the answer choice is wrong. The longer and more complex the fact pattern, the easier it is for you to make a factual mistake by the time you reach the answer choices. If you notice you make this kind of error when choosing answers for long fact patterns, break up the fact pattern by marking up and making notes in the margins.[31] Look for practice questions with long fact patterns to practice these skills.

Take a look at the following question to see how an incorrect answer choice can mischaracterize the facts from the fact pattern.

Johann gave Alicia an engagement ring for Valentine's Day. Six months later Johann called off the engagement but told Alicia that she could keep the ring. Alicia did not want to wear the ring anymore, so she put the ring in a small box, which she taped closed. She then put the box on the top shelf of her closet for safekeeping. A year later Alicia moved to another apartment, forgetting that the ring was on the shelf. The new tenant, Darla, found the ring when she was moving in and showed it to the landlord.

At common law, the engagement ring belongs to

a. Darla as the finder because Alicia abandoned the ring when she decided to leave the ring in her old apartment.

b. Darla as the finder because Alicia lost the ring when she left it on the shelf.

c. Alicia because she mislaid the ring when she deliberately put it away on the shelf and forgot it.

d. the landlord because Alicia mislaid the ring and the landlord does not know how to contact Alicia.

---

31. See Part Two, Chapter 10.

This question's correct answer depends on whether the ring should be classified as lost, mislaid, or abandoned property.[32] A careful reading of the facts in the choices, however, would eliminate several of the choices even if you were not clear about the proper rules.

For instance, in answer (a), the phrase "when she decided to leave the ring in her old apartment" is factually incorrect because the fact pattern does not explicitly indicate that Alicia made such a decision. So, answer (a) *mischaracterizes* the facts in the fact pattern. Similarly, answer (d) *adds* facts that are not in the fact pattern. Nothing in the facts says that the landlord does not know how to contact Alicia.[33] And finally, answer (b) provides *incomplete facts* for its rule. (For property to be lost, the owner must not only leave the item, but leave the item accidentally, making it unlikely that they would remember where they put it.) The correct answer, then, is (c) because the facts in answer (c) both satisfy the rule and do not misrepresent the facts in the fact pattern.

Note also that it is easy to misread the answer choices when you have a series of questions based on the same fact pattern. For instance, if your law school exam says "questions 1-3 are based on the following fact pattern," you have to remember the facts when answering question 3 just as clearly as you did when answering question 1. But in the meantime, you have read and answered questions 1 and 2, diluting your recollection of the fact pattern.

If you frequently choose wrong answers for questions based on fact patterns with multiple questions, you must pay particular attention to the call of each question. Scan the calls of the question for each question *before* you read the fact pattern. For example, if you circle or underline the parties identified in the calls of the question, you will know to focus on those same actors when you read the fact pattern. Underline or circle those same parties in the fact patterns as you are reading to keep you on topic.

---

32. At common law, abandoned property belongs to the finder. Lost property belongs to the true owner or, if the true owner doesn't claim it, to the finder. Mislaid property belongs to the true owner or, if the true owner cannot be found, to the owner of the property on which the item is found.

33. If you were supposed to treat the phrase "and the landlord does not know how to contact Alicia" as a fact, it would have been in the fact pattern *or* the call of the question. It is common for professors to add facts to the call of the question, only for that question.

Another danger of fact patterns with multiple questions is that any question based on the single fact pattern may add facts to the fact pattern *only for that question*, which can increase your chances of misreading the facts in the *next* question's answers. These questions with additional facts often begin, "Assuming only for question 2 that XYZ happened . . ."[34] In our experience, many students panic when reading fact patterns with multiple questions, and so they are less careful when reading the facts in the answer choices. Or sometimes they assume that because the fact pattern covers several questions, they don't need to go back and read the details of the fact pattern when answering questions 2 and 3. Do not fall into these traps; read the facts in these answer choices as carefully as you would the facts in a single question's answers. Also, slow down when reading fact patterns for multiple questions. If there are three questions based on the fact pattern, you can take three times as long to read the fact pattern as you would for a one-question fact pattern, or you can go back to check the key details.

MISREADING THE LEGAL RULE

Misreading the rule in an answer choice often is not really a reading problem—it is usually a substantive knowledge problem. In other words, rather than simply choosing the incorrect version because you read it too quickly, you chose an incorrect phrasing of the rule because you aren't exactly sure what the correct rule on that topic really is.[35] When you know the law, it is much harder for exam writers to distract you with incorrect versions of the rule in the answers.

Nonetheless, there are answer choices that contain *incomplete versions of the rule* or that *leave out key words* that make them an incorrect answer choice. When you read such answers too quickly, your brain may fill in the missing pieces or words from the correct statement of that rule, leading you to choose the wrong answer.

---

34. While these kinds of questions have been eliminated on the MBE, they may still be used in law school exams since professors are familiar with this style of questions.

35. Sometimes this confusion comes from your professors using shorthand for the rules in class. See Chapter 19 on rules for further explanations on the dangers of the shorthand version of rules.

For example, look at the following contracts call of the question and possible answer.[36]

> Assuming that there was an enforceable contract between Tom and Chris and that Chris breached the contract, which of the following remedies is a court most likely to grant?
>
> a. All consequential damages proximately caused by the breach

If you read that answer choice quickly, you might assume that it is a correct statement of the potential remedy for a contract because you are assuming an additional word in the answer that isn't there. The correct statement would be this.

> a. All *foreseeable* consequential damages proximately caused by the breach.

Here's another example for a criminal law question.

> Which of the following statements is Herman's best defense against battery charges?
>
> a. Herman may use nondeadly force to prevent a trespass or taking.

Here the answer once again is incorrect because it omits key words from the rule that a hurried reader may not notice. The answer with the correct rule would read like so.

---

36. You don't need the fact pattern here because the answers are only about rules.

> a. Herman may use *reasonable* nondeadly force to prevent an *imminent* trespass or taking.

Always be wary of answer choices that fail to give you the complete rules—don't assume the exam drafters omitted those words by accident. Always read answers carefully to be sure they contain the full applicable rule (or the applicable part of the rule if the question is asking about only one element of a legal issue).[37]

Finally, although it is not technically a misreading problem, beware of answers containing gratuitous legalese, especially Latin words. When law students are reading quickly and they see four answer choices, including one that contains a Latin word or phrase, they sometimes choose that answer because it just "sounds right." Phrases like "res ipsa loquitur," "quantum meruit," "parens patriae," or even "estoppel," while impressive sounding and sometimes intimidating, are no more correct than their plain English language counterparts. They are often included as red herrings, so do not make this psychological reading mistake! If you know the law, you will know whether that phrase or doctrine is applicable to and answers correctly the question you are reading.

IGNORING WORDS THAT INDICATE CONDITIONS OR NARROW CHOICES

Many multiple-choice answers contain words that *set conditions or narrow choices*. These words indicate the parameters and/or limitations (factual and/or legal) under which an answer may be correct or incorrect. These include words such as

if, only if, and, or, unless, because, since, must, may, cannot, not

---

37. Note also that this is why it is critical that you include *complete rules in your outlines* rather than shorthand versions so that you don't get used to filling in the missing elements in your mind. We discuss this further in Chapter 19.

Taking this kind of language into account is critical to picking the best answer choice, but students often miss or ignore these limitations as they rush to complete the questions, and consequently they choose the wrong answer.

Words that indicate cause or condition

First, let's look at words that state the conditions under which an answer is the correct choice. These include both direct causal words, such as "because" and "since," and limiting conditional words, such as "if," "only if," and "unless."

When drafters use causal words such as "because" or "since" in their answer choices, they mean that the explanation following the answer is the *reason* the answer is true, either in terms of facts, rules, or a combination of both, depending on the nature of the question. In contrast, when drafters use conditional words such as "if" or "unless" in their answer choices, they mean that the answer is true *only* under those specific factual and/or legal circumstances. Without those circumstances, the answer would never be true.

Take a look at the following example.

After Ted accidentally cut Gary off at an intersection, Ted and Gary both pulled over to the side of the road and got out of their cars. Gary began yelling at Ted and then shoved Ted hard. The two men then began to fight. Soon Ted was on the ground, and Gary began punching Ted hard in the face. At that point, Joe, who had been watching the fist fight, pointed a gun at Gary and yelled, "Stop punching him or I'll shoot you!"

If Gary sues Joe for assault, will Gary prevail?

a. Yes, because Joe threatened to use deadly force against Gary.
b. No, since Gary was the original aggressor.
c. Yes, unless Joe was related to Ted.
d. No, if it was apparent that Gary was about to inflict serious bodily harm upon Ted.

All four of the answers here have conditional or causal words that qualify the word "yes" or "no" at the beginning of the answer choice. Here, if you first read the call of the question, you would know that this is a torts question involving assault (and not criminal assault because Gary is suing Joe). For Gary to prevail, the elements of an assault claim must be satisfied by the facts *and* Joe must not have any viable defenses.[38]

Here, answer (a) contains the causal word "because," meaning that what follows is the reason the conclusion is correct in terms of fact and/or law. In answer (a), "yes" means all the elements of assault are satisfied by the facts and no defenses apply because Joe threatened to use deadly force. But a threat of deadly force does not prevent Joe from asserting a defense of others or self-defense, so it does not explain why Gary's claim could succeed. (Moreover, this answer is incorrect as a factual matter because the facts are unclear whether punching someone in the face is deadly force.[39])

In answer (b) we have the same problem with the qualifier "since." Like the word "because," "since" means that what follows is the reason the answer choice is correct in terms of the facts and/or law. Here, the question of who the original aggressor was in the fight between Gary and Ted has nothing to do with the elements required to prove Joe's assault on Gary or with Joe's defenses to the assault. Therefore, who the aggressor is cannot be the *reason* for Joe being able to defend against Gary's assault claim, even if it is factually true that Gary pushed Ted first.

Answer (c) uses the conditional word "unless," which means that the *only* way Gary will not prevail is if Joe was related to Ted. Here, Joe being related to Ted is not legally relevant to assault. Further, Gary will not prevail if Joe was defending Ted. So (c) cannot be the correct choice.

---

38. Note here that the call of the question is "will Gary prevail," which includes a consideration of possible defenses, as opposed to "can Gary state a claim," which would only require you to consider whether the elements of assault are satisfied.

39. While punching someone in the face might arguably be deadly force, multiple-choice questions tend to make this much clearer to make the analysis simpler. Thus, deadly force usually means a knife or a gun or something obvious. Because Joe's use of force must be reasonable—i.e., roughly equivalent to Gary's use of force—this is an important factual distinction.

This leaves us with the correct answer, (d), which contains the conditional word "if." "If" provides the key fact(s) and legal element(s) missing from the fact pattern that would allow Joe to claim a defense of others. A defense of others is permissible when the assault was reasonable under the circumstances to protect another. Adding "it was apparent that Gary was about to inflict serious bodily harm upon Ted" gives us the missing fact to see that Joe acted reasonably under the circumstances to protect Ted.

Thus, when you see the words "if" or "only if," be aware that it won't be the correct choice if there are still missing facts or elements that the "if" statement does not address. For instance, the answer

> No, if Joe was a licensed gun owner.

would be incorrect because adding the fact that Joe was a licensed gun owner has nothing to do with whether it was reasonable for Joe to try to defend Ted from Gary's physical attack.

The "and" versus "or" trap

Confusing whether the parts in an answer are *alternatives* ("or") or *requirements* ("and") is an easy mistake to make when reading quickly, but failing to see this distinction can lead students to choose the wrong answer.

For example, look at the following question and possible answer.

> To show the statute is unconstitutional, the plaintiff must argue that
>
> a. the statute does not promote a compelling governmental interest and there are less restrictive means of achieving the government's interest.

A quick reading of this answer choice looks like it would be the right choice for a fact pattern containing a statute that discriminates on the basis of race. At first glance, a student would remember that to be constitutional, such a statute must survive strict scrutiny, which is a two-part test: the statute must promote a compelling governmental interest *and* it must be the least restrictive means to achieve those interests. However, the question here is how can a *plaintiff* prove it is unconstitutional. If the plaintiff succeeds in arguing that *either* prong of the test is absent, the plaintiff will prevail. Therefore, this answer is incorrect. The correct answer would be

> b. The statute does not promote a compelling governmental interest *or* there are less restrictive means of achieving the government's interest.

These two answers are exactly the same but for the words "and" and "or," but that word in the context of the question determines which of the two answers is correct. Always ask yourself whether the answer is dealing with *alternatives* ("or") or *requirements* ("and") when making your choice.

Mandatory versus discretionary words

Often the correct answer choice will turn on the particular auxiliary or helping verb used in the answer choices. These words are

must, may, can, should, and their negatives (cannot, must not, etc.).

They indicate whether the action verb in the answer is a requirement or is merely a permissible option. The words "may" and "can" indicate *options*, while the words "must" and "cannot" indicate *requirements*.[40] The word "should" usually indicates *more than an option but less than a*

---

40. "Must not" and "can never" are also absolutes and indicate that there is nothing optional about the answer.

requirement[41]; it is a preference for or recommendation of an option. It is easy to become distracted by an incorrect answer choice that contains the correct rule but the incorrect helping verb. If you find that you are missing multiple-choice questions because you are not paying close enough attention to the helping verbs in the answer choices, circle these verbs to help you focus your attention on those key words.

To illustrate, in the following civil procedure question, the helping verbs are the key to selecting the correct answer choice.

> Plaintiff, who lives in Los Angeles, has no health insurance. On vacation in Wyoming, defendant, who lives in Laramie, Wyoming, hits plaintiff with defendant's car. As a result of these injuries, plaintiff incurs $150,000 in medical bills.
>
> If plaintiff decides to sue defendant for damages, which of the following statements is true?
>
> a. Plaintiff must sue defendant in federal district court in California.
> b. Plaintiff may sue defendant in federal district court in Wyoming.
> c. Plaintiff must sue defendant in federal district court in Wyoming.
> d. Plaintiff must sue defendant in Wyoming state court.

In this diversity jurisdiction question, answers (b) and (c) are virtually identical except for the helping verbs "must" and "may." Because you can see that the amount involved is large enough to permit bringing a diversity claim in federal district court, you should be able to rule out answer (d) because it contains the word "must" and not "may."

If you know your diversity jurisdiction rules, you know that a suit *may* be brought in federal court when you have a plaintiff and a defendant from two different states and the amount in question is sufficient. But this does not *require* the plaintiff to bring suit in federal court—it is merely an

---

41. For example, an answer choice saying "The plaintiff *should* file in federal court in California because . . ." would be stating that even though California is not required, it is the preferable or recommended location for the lawsuit.

option. Therefore, answers (a) and (c) are incorrect, and answer (b) is the right answer. Choosing the correct answer here depends on knowing that rule (the substantive knowledge) and paying careful attention to the helping verbs.

TIME TO EVALUATE

Look at the questions you missed on your practice test to see whether you have made the following kinds of misreading errors when selecting an answer choice.

1. **Did you choose an incorrect answer because you misread the facts in the answer?**

2. **Did you choose an incorrect answer because you misread the legal rule contained in the answer?**

   If you answered "yes" to either question above:

   • Work on your time management during the exam so you have the time to carefully read the answer choices. For most students, slowing down solves a simple misreading problem.

   • Follow The Approach so that you have an exam strategy to complete the exam and only review the questions where you are unsure your answer choice is correct.

3. **Did you choose an incorrect answer because you did not pay attention to words that indicate conditions or narrowed choices?**

   If you answered "yes" to this question:

   • Identify the language patterns in the answers that are throwing you off. Look for similarities and trends.

   • Pay special attention to those language patterns and circle or underline them in your answer choices when you take your next multiple-choice practice exam.

A FINAL NOTE ON MISREADING THE ANSWER CHOICES

If you are misreading the answer choices, working on your time management during the exam, following The Approach, and identifying the language patterns in the answers that are throwing you off will correct the problem. Keep these skills in mind and take your next practice test. If, however, you seem to understand the answer choices but are still having reading issues when choosing the correct answer, read the next chapter.

CHAPTER 16

Did I Misread the Fact Pattern?

When you misread the fact pattern, you are likely making one or two common mistakes.

1. You are *assuming* the fact pattern contains facts that are not actually there.

2. You are *ignoring or failing to see* some of the legally relevant facts that have been included in the fact pattern.

Here we are assuming that you know the law and are actually making a reading error—not a substantive knowledge error. That said, the better you know the law, the more likely it is that you will recognize the legal significance of any facts given or omitted.

ASSUMING FACTS NOT PRESENT IN THE FACT PATTERN

Here's an example where a student might assume facts that are not actually included.

On his seventeenth birthday, Tony bought a motorcycle from Greg's Cycle Shop. The motorcycle's price was $10,000. Tony gave Greg's Cycle Shop $3000 in cash and signed an agreement stating that he would pay the rest in monthly installments of $250 until he had paid off the balance. Three months later, however, Tony stopped paying Greg's Cycle Shop any more money for the motorcycle because he lost his part-time job. Greg's Cycle Shop is suing Tony for the remaining payments.

Assuming the age of majority is 18, Tony is

a. liable for the market value of the motorcycle.
b. liable for the rest of the payments.
c. not liable for the rest of the payments because Tony's age when he signed the contract relieves him of liability for the remaining payments.
d. not liable because Tony disaffirmed the contract.

In this contracts question, you should know this is about a minor's liability for a contract because of Tony's age given in the fact pattern and because the call of the question flags it as relevant. Knowing that minors can void contracts they signed when they were minors, you might be tempted to choose answer (c) or (d), which relieve Tony of liability. Nowhere in the fact pattern, however, does it say that Tony actively disaffirmed the contract—it merely says that he stopped making payments. The fact pattern also doesn't say that Tony returned the motorcycle, which he would have to do to disaffirm the contract. If you read this fact pattern too quickly, you might *assume* that Tony disaffirmed the contract when the facts say he stopped making payments. Assuming facts are given *when they have not actually been provided* will cause you to select an incorrect answer choice.[42]

---

42. The correct answer here is (b), liable for the rest of the payments (at least until he disaffirms the contract and returns the motorcycle).

FAILING TO SEE LEGALLY RELEVANT FACTS

Failing to note a key fact provided in a fact pattern, on the other hand, occurs most often when a fact pattern is particularly long and complex. For example, read through the next criminal law question.

Linda had always admired her elderly friend and next-door neighbor Sandra's diamond necklace. Sandra had a weak heart and bad eyesight, and Linda often went to Sandra's house to do chores that were too difficult for Sandra to perform. When Sandra left to go visit her daughter for a week, she gave Linda a key to Sandra's home in case there was any emergency while Sandra was gone.

That night Linda woke up thinking Sandra's diamond necklace would look wonderful with the gown Linda had bought for an important upcoming charity event the following evening. Linda got up and took the house key that Sandra had given her and went over to Sandra's house to borrow the necklace for the event. Unfortunately, Linda discovered that Sandra had accidentally given her the wrong key, so Linda was not able to open Sandra's front door. Determined to find a way into the house, Linda found an unlatched window in the basement, opened it, and crawled in.

Linda went into Sandra's bedroom and took the necklace case from the place where she knew Sandra kept it. Unknown to Linda, Sandra's trip to see her daughter had been postponed and Sandra was still at home. As Linda turned to leave Sandra's bedroom with the necklace, Sandra walked out of the bathroom, saw a hazy figure in her bedroom, suffered a heart attack, and died.

Which of the following crimes has Linda committed?

a. Burglary
b. Burglary and larceny
c. Burglary, larceny, and felony murder
d. None of the above

Under these facts, to be guilty of any of the crimes listed in the answer choices, Linda must have intended to deprive Sandra of her necklace permanently. Stuck in the middle of the second paragraph of the facts, however, it says that Linda wanted "to borrow the necklace for the event." Nowhere do the facts provide information to suggest Linda planned to keep the necklace permanently. Thus, (d) would be the correct answer here. A student reading through this problem quickly might not notice that key phrase, and then instead the student would be running through all the elements of each crime to see whether they were satisfied, wasting valuable time and leading to the selection of an incorrect response.

To avoid misreading the fact pattern, you want to be sure you are circling or underlining *key facts that have legal significance.* Facts have legal significance when they trigger legal issues: These can be basic legal issues, special rules, or exceptions or defenses to the rule. If you know the law, you should know how to recognize these legally significant facts. By circling the words that trigger legal issues, you can go back over the fact pattern quickly to see whether all the required elements for the triggered issues, special rules, defenses, or exceptions have been satisfied by the fact pattern.

Here are some examples.

Facts that trigger basic legal issues

"David and Yolanda signed their agreement stating that David would build her website."

Here you would circle or underline the words "signed" and "agreement" because these words may trigger a *statute of frauds issue* in contracts.

"Virginia aimed and fired a single shot through Terry's heart."

Here you would circle or underline "aimed and fired a single shot through Terry's heart" because these words should suggest the issue of *premeditation* for first-degree murder in criminal law.

Facts that trigger special rules

"Paulo had a business selling computer accessories online."

If this is in a contracts question, you would circle or underline the words "business selling" because they may indicate that contract *rules for merchants* are at issue.

"Five-year-old Jaden ran over Mrs. Murphy's foot while riding his bicycle."

Here you would underline "five-year-old" and "ran over" because liability for injuries may be different for *minors* than for adults.[43]

Facts that trigger exceptions to the rule

"In response to a subpoena, Dennis returned to Hawaii to testify in court. While there, he was served with a Complaint for damages for an unrelated traffic accident."

Here, for a civil procedure question you would circle or underline "in response to a subpoena" because there is *no personal jurisdiction* over a defendant via presence in the state when the defendant was brought into the state involuntarily by subpoena.

"Although Doug knew Carmen hated to be tickled, he grabbed her from behind and tickled her as a joke."

For a torts question, you would circle or underline "Doug knew" because a defendant's knowledge of a plaintiff's special sensitivity triggers a *subjective standard* in determining what constitutes a harmful or offensive touching for battery.

---

43. Age also may trigger special rules in contracts, as we saw with the 17-year-old motorcycle purchaser.

Facts that trigger defenses to the rule

"Jim had five beers during happy hour before getting into his car to drive home."

Here you want to circle or underline "five beers during happy hour" as these facts may indicate *voluntary intoxication*, which is not a defense to first-degree murder.

"The store's security guard brought Pat to the back office and left her there while he got the store manager."

Here you would circle the words "store's security guard" and "store manager" because these facts would trigger a *merchant's defense* to a false imprisonment claim.

TIME TO EVALUATE

Look at the questions you missed on your practice test to see whether you have made the following kinds of misreading errors when reading the fact pattern.

1. **Did you assume facts in the fact pattern that *are not actually there*?**

   If you answered "yes" to this question:

   - Work on your time management during the exam so you have the time to carefully read the fact pattern. For most students, slowing down solves a simple misreading problem.

   - Follow The Approach so that you have an exam strategy to complete the exam and only review the questions where you are unsure your answer choice is correct.

2. **Did you *ignore or fail to see* some of the legally relevant facts that are contained in the fact pattern?**

   If you answered "yes" to this question:

   - Work on identifying the key facts that trigger legal issues.

- Circle or underline those facts in the fact pattern and compare these facts to the facts identified in the explanation for the correct answer.

A FINAL NOTE ON MISREADING THE FACT PATTERN

If you are misreading the fact pattern because you erroneously assume facts in the fact pattern, working on your time management during the exam and following The Approach will, for most students, correct the problem.

If you are misreading the fact pattern because you are ignoring the key facts that are relevant to the issue, taking the steps of identifying, then circling or underlining the key facts in the fact pattern and comparing them to the facts in the answer explanation will generally correct the problem. However, in taking a practice exam, if you do not understand *why* the trigger facts listed in the explanation *are* the key facts, then you have more than a reading problem; you have a substantive knowledge problem, and you should read the next chapter.

IF YOU HAVE A READING PROBLEM—A FINAL SUMMARY

At this point, you should be able to determine whether you are

1. misreading the calls of the question,

2. misreading the answer choices, and/or

3. misreading the fact patterns.

If you are misreading any of the above, then you want to do the following.

- Check your time allocations to be sure you are giving yourself enough time to read the entire question carefully.

- Look for trends and similarities in the questions you misread to identify your specific weaknesses.

- Practice reading calls of the question to determine what you are being asked to decide and what role you are assuming.

- Circle or underline key words in the answer choices that you are misreading, including words that indicate conditions or words that narrow choices.

- Circle or underline key facts in the fact pattern that trigger legal issues and add them to your outline. (See Chapter 21.)

CHAPTER 17

Do I Have a Substantive Knowledge Problem?

If you have read Chapters 13 through 16 and determined that you do not have a reading problem, but you are still failing to choose the correct answers when taking a multiple-choice exam, then you have a problem with your substantive knowledge of the law. And if you have identified and corrected your reading problems but are still choosing the wrong multiple-choice answer, then you also have a problem with your substantive knowledge of the law.[44] The gaps in your substantive knowledge may be all in one subject area, such as contracts, or you may have a broader problem—for example, you may be unable to define or distinguish sub-elements, defenses, or exceptions to rules in many areas of law.[45]

By saying you have a substantive knowledge problem, we mean that *you do not know or understand the legal issues and rules well enough to be able to apply them* to identify the correct answer.

Take a look once again at the questions we asked you at the beginning of Chapter 13.

---

44. As we said before, many students find that they both misread questions and have substantive knowledge deficiencies. Both problems are correctable, but you need to tackle them one at a time.

45. Substantive knowledge problems can be a bigger problem for students on multiple-choice tests than on essay tests because students have no opportunity to explain their answers on a multiple-choice test to receive partial credit.

- Do I miss questions in many different areas of the subject matter being tested?

- Do I get the correct answer when I am able to read the facts and the questions and answers slowly?

If the answer to one or both of these questions is "no," then you probably had gaps in your substantive knowledge when you took the practice test. As we note in Chapter 13, for law students, if almost all of the questions you missed on your property test were future interests questions, then you have a gap in your substantive knowledge of property. For bar students, if most of the questions you missed on the MBE practice test were contracts questions, but not property or torts, then you have gaps in your substantive knowledge of contracts. In both situations, the substantive gaps are impairing your multiple-choice test performance.

In addition, you have a substantive knowledge problem if adding extra time to answer questions does not increase the number of correct answers you can identify. No amount of time in the world can correct for a lack of knowledge. Moreover, if you don't understand why an answer you chose is correct or incorrect after reviewing the explanation for the correct answer given by a workbook or a professor, you definitely have a substantive knowledge problem.[46]

You may think that you just need to go over all your outlines again, in their totality. Don't do it! Your gaps in knowledge are generally much smaller than the areas you know—so you may be spending 80 percent of your time going over stuff you already know and feeling really good

---

46. The only exception to this may occur when a professor or bar examiners include a poorly drafted or inaccurate question in the mix. Remember, the MBE contains new questions that the bar examiners include on the exam to see whether they are good questions to use in the future—they won't actually count in your score. Similarly, many law schools give their professors a statistical analysis of students' answers to tell professors whether they have used poorly drafted or incorrect questions. Law professors may take this analysis into account when grading these exams and discount poorly drafted questions. Unfortunately, in either case you will not know which questions, if any, these are.

about yourself, while only spending 20 percent of your time on the stuff you really need to study.

Instead, just feel good about yourself right now. If you know more than you don't know (51 percent or more), you should feel good about yourself.[47] Now forget that, and focus 100 percent of your time on the stuff you need to know but don't know. Once you feel roughly competent in all the subject areas you need, *then* you can go back to studying everything.

THE "GAPS" OUTLINE

If your problem on multiple-choice tests is exclusively or primarily a substantive knowledge problem,[48] then the first thing you need to do is *identify the specific areas of law where you chose the wrong answers.* This means you must take these two steps.

1. Make a list of the subject areas where you appear to have a substantive knowledge deficiency.

2. Then list the sub-topics within each subject area where you missed the correct answer.

   Be as specific as you can about identifying the gaps in your substantive knowledge.

For example, for law students, the gap can be on specific topics such as homicide in criminal law. For MBE exam takers, are the gaps in just one subject, say torts? Or are they in torts and evidence? Once you have

---

47. If you know less than 50 percent of what you need to know, you should feel hopeful. Feel hopeful that you will soon feel good about yourself.
48. This assumes you've already worked to correct reading problems.

identified the specific areas of law and topics where you are having difficulties, you should do the following.

Make a list of substantive knowledge gaps

For example:

For Law Students	For Bar Students

Criminal Law (area of law)
  1) Homicide (specific topic)
  2) Conspiracy (specific topic)
	Torts (area of law)
	  1) Intentional Torts (specific topic)
	
	Evidence (area of law)
	  1) Hearsay (specific topic)

Once you have identified the overall area(s) and specific topics of the law with which you are struggling, the next question is: Are you missing questions throughout that subject area, or are there specific subtopics where you consistently choose incorrect answers? For example, of your missed answers on homicide, are most of them about premeditation?

Here we are looking for questions you missed because of a lack of knowledge, so you are looking for a pattern of missed questions. Usually it will be obvious to you where your substantive knowledge is weak. If you aren't sure whether you have a substantive knowledge problem with a particular topic or sub-topic, however, take the time to review *all* the questions on that topic, including the ones you answered correctly. By the law of averages, sometimes you will choose a correct answer just by sheer luck. If you don't fully understand the explanations for the *correct* answers on that topic, that lack of understanding will confirm that you need to work on your substantive knowledge for that issue.

List the subtopics within each subject area

For example:

For Law Students	For Bar Students

Criminal Law (area of law)
  1) Homicide (specific topic)
    • Premeditation (sub-topic)
  2) Conspiracy (specific topic)
	Torts (area of law)
	  1) Intentional Torts (specific topic)
	
	Evidence (area of law)
	  1) Hearsay (specific topic)
	    • Double Hearsay (sub-topic)

Now let's look at what you've written down. Putting this list together gives you an *outline of the gaps in your substantive knowledge*. This outline tells you which areas of your substantive law outlines need revisions and which specific topics (and subtopics) within those areas of law are incorrect or incomplete.

WHY REVISE OUTLINES?

At this point students often ask us: "Why go back to the outlines? I've identified the problem issues and read the explanations for the answers I've gotten wrong. Isn't that enough?"[49] In our experience, for many students this is not enough; if you are reading this book, merely reading what the correct answers are probably has not worked for you.

You go back to your outline because that is where you have recorded your understanding of the law. It is this *incomplete* understanding of the law that is affecting your multiple-choice test performance. By figuring out and correcting what is missing, incomplete, or wrong in your outline, you

---

49. Students often assume incorrectly that merely by reading correct answers they will recall the correct law for an exam question on the same topic when the time comes.

will correct and deepen your understanding of the law. This is the key to improving your performance on a multiple-choice test—you will be able to choose the right answer *only* when you know the law.

By "know the law" here, we mean more than simply memorizing the rules listed in your outline.

Knowing the law includes

- being able to recognize the fact scenarios that give rise to that legal issue;

- being able to recall the rule for that legal issue in detail, including its elements and sub-elements; and

- knowing how that rule applies in a variety of factual circumstances.[50]

If this looks familiar, it should. These are the steps of basic legal analysis, or IRAC.

Every multiple-choice question requires you to

- identify the legal *Issue* in the question;

- recall the applicable *Rule* for that issue; and to

- determine how the rule *Applies* to those facts, in order to reach the correct

- *Conclusion.*

---

50. In our opinion, every law school outline should IRAC the substantive material: identify the **I**ssue, state the **R**ules for the issue, and include examples of how the rule was **A**pplied to facts in prior cases and class hypotheticals. By categorizing the application into examples that satisfy the rule and examples that do not satisfy the rule ("Is/Is not"), the **C**onclusions to those examples are also reflected in the outline. If your outlines do not contain this information, you will have a harder time analyzing legal issues in both multiple-choice and essay exams.

If you are getting an answer wrong, you are reaching the wrong conclusion because of a substantive knowledge problem.

To understand why you are reaching the wrong conclusion, you must
ask yourself

- Did I miss the *Issue* in the fact pattern?

- Did I miss the *Rule* for that issue?

- Did I miss the *Application* of the rule to the fact pattern?

Always analyze your incorrect answer by looking first for the issue (I),
then the rule (R), and then the application (A). Once you have reached a
step where you find an error, stop and correct that problem on your
outline. Only after you have corrected that problem should you move
on to see whether there is a problem in the next step. We do it this way
because if you cannot identify the correct *issue*, then you will not know
what *rule* to apply and cannot select the correct answer. If you spotted the
correct *issue* but don't know the *rule*, then again, you cannot select the
correct answer. And if you spotted the correct *issue* and know the *rule* but
cannot *apply* it, you still won't select the correct answer.

Warning: *Do not assume the problem is always with Step 2, the Rule.* Very
often students can recite the Rule but cannot spot the Issue, or they make
mistakes in the Application step. For example, in property, most students
can memorize and recite RAP—the Rule Against Perpetuities. An interest is
void if there is any possibility that it may vest more than 21 years after some
life in being at the creation of the interest. What the student may not know is
what a RAP problem looks like *factually*. You need to be able to spot the issue
before you can identify the correct rule and then apply it.

Now let's look at each of these steps individually to see how you would
identify the problem, how you would take the necessary steps to correct
each problem in your outline, and how you would apply this to your
multiple-choice exams.

CHAPTER 18

Did I Miss the *Issue* in the Fact Pattern?

ISSUE SPOTTING? ON A MULTIPLE-CHOICE EXAM? DOES IT MATTER?

While law students understand that issue spotting is a major component on an essay exam, they often believe it is not a required skill for multiple-choice exams. After all, they tell us, the potential issues raised in a fact pattern are identified in the call of the question and/or in the multiple-choice answers. They think that as long as they know the rules for every issue, they can simply apply the rules for the issues identified in the answers to the facts in the question to arrive at the correct answer.

Even with multiple-choice questions, however, issue spotting is a required skill for two reasons. First, you simply don't have enough time to test every potential rule raised in the answers against the facts; you need to be able to eliminate off-topic answers quickly, so you must be able to issue-spot effectively as you read the fact pattern. Second, some topics in the calls of the question are broad enough that you may not know what rule to apply. For example, "Is it admissible?" "Does the court have juris-diction?" and "What is the best defense?" are some questions where the issue is not clear from the call of the question. It is your issue-spotting skills that help you narrow the answer choices to the issue raised by the fact pattern.

Students who include only rules in their outlines often cannot recognize what fact patterns trigger the legal issue to which the rule applies. These students memorize the rules, but they don't really understand when they come into play, particularly when they are reading quickly. We test whether students can spot an issue in a fact pattern by asking them to give us a hypothetical that might trigger the rule or a sub-element of the rule. If you cannot think of a hypothetical illustrating where that rule might be applied, then you aren't likely to be able to spot that issue on an exam.

Students often tell us their outlines will become too long to be a useful study tool if they include every possible trigger fact for every issue. But that is not what we are asking you to do here. We recommend adding trigger facts for *only those issues that you are missing on practice exams.* If you have not yet taken practice exams, include trigger facts from cases and professor hypotheticals from your class notes. Use this technique to improve and revise only the weak points in your knowledge. This is much more efficient than adding them for issues that you have already mastered.

Remember that on multiple-choice questions, the exam drafters have to write questions that have one clear correct answer; there is no room for discussion or debate. This means that for each issue there is a limited set of facts that will clearly trigger that legal issue with only one correct answer choice. Consequently, the same kinds of fact patterns or trigger facts for a given issue appear over and over on multiple-choice exams. Once you've identified the trigger facts, you can add them to your outline and memorize them just as you memorized the rules and sub-rules[51] for the issue. Identify and memorize these key trigger facts, and you've mastered the I step of IRAC.

WHAT IS A "TRIGGER FACT"?

Trigger facts are the specific facts in the multiple-choice fact pattern that should alert you that a legal issue or sub-issue is in play. For example, one of

---

51. By a sub-rule here we mean a rule that explains or defines one of the main elements for a rule.

the requirements for common law burglary is that the theft must occur at night.[52] This is a clear trigger fact: Any multiple-choice fact pattern about burglary *must* contain a phrase telling you the theft took place at night in order to be a potential common law burglary question. The question will either use that exact phrase, "at night," or it will give you a time that is clearly at night, such as 10 p.m.[53] Similarly, a phrase such as "A decided to kill B" constitutes trigger facts for the legal issue of premeditation for a homicide question.

ISSUE-SPOTTING PROBLEMS

Students have several different kinds of problems with issue spotting that need to be addressed differently on the revised outlines. They include the following common problems.

Common Problems with Issue Spotting

- Students fail to recognize the key facts that raised the issue.

- Students erroneously relate the key facts of an issue to the wrong issue.

- Students see an issue that was not raised in the fact pattern.

To see how to identify and correct these issue-spotting problems, take a look at the following multiple-choice question.

---

52. Common law burglary is defined as the breaking and entering of the dwelling of another at night with intent to commit a felony therein.

53. In contrast, on an essay exam the professor might include facts saying "at 6 p.m." or "at dusk" or "in the early morning." This might require you to discuss whether the theft actually occurred at night, requiring you to compare and contrast common law burglary with modern law burglary.

In response to research showing that children do better educationally, emotionally, and economically when they live in two-parent families, the state legislature of East Carolina has passed a statute stating that "in order to obtain a divorce, all couples with minor children must first attend a one-week course outlining the negative effects of divorce on children." The purpose of the statute is to "encourage married couples with children to stay married for the benefit of their children." The cost of the required class is $500, which must be paid by the party filing for divorce.

Sophia and Walter are married and have two children: Amy, age four, and Danny, age seven. Both Sophia and Walter worked minimum-wage jobs, and they use food stamps to scrape enough together to support the family. Lately Walter has been drinking too much, so he lost his job. As a result, he has become depressed and verbally abusive toward Sophia. Sophia wants to file for divorce, but she doesn't have the money to attend the week-long class required by the statute.

If Sophia sues to challenge the East Carolina statute, the court is likely to rule the statute is

a. unconstitutional, because married couples with children are being treated differently than married couples without children.
b. constitutional, because protecting the interests of children is a compelling governmental interest.
c. constitutional, because the state's power as *parens patriae* provides a compelling interest in protecting children.
d. unconstitutional, because the state provides no mechanism, such as a fee waiver, for poor married parents to obtain a divorce.

Here, while it is clear from the answer choices that this is a constitutional law question, neither the call of the question nor the answer choices provide obvious clues as to what kind of constitutional issue or analysis is at stake. In other words, the answers do not say things such as "substantive due process," "equal protection," "first amendment," or "fourth amendment." Consequently, you must be able to identify the trigger facts in the fact pattern to be able to know what *kind* of constitutional analysis is required.

If you recognized the trigger facts, however, you could immediately narrow your choices and select the right answer. The trigger fact here is that the statute concerns marriage and divorce. These facts immediately signal that this is a constitutional question involving a fundamental right, the right of privacy, which includes issues of marriage (and divorce) and procreation. Knowing that this is a question about impinging on a fundamental right tells you which analysis from your constitutional law outline to apply—substantive due process. Your outline should tell you that to uphold a statute that impinges on a fundamental right, the court must have a compelling governmental interest, and the statute must be narrowly tailored to achieve its goals. Here, then, the correct answer is (d) because even if the state's interest in protecting children from the negative effects of divorce is a compelling state interest, the statute is not narrowly tailored to achieve these ends.[54]

Now let's look at the kinds of issue-spotting errors a student might make and discuss how to revise the outline to correct these problems.

FAILING TO RECOGNIZE KEY FACTS THAT RAISE THE ISSUE

Assume here that a student chose answer (c) because she failed to understand the significance of the trigger facts, and answer (c) sounded good because it had constitutional language (compelling interest) and legalese (*parens patriae*). When you miss a question because you failed to spot the correct issue, you want to *add those facts to your outline as an example of what that issue looks like* so that you will recognize which issue those kinds of facts trigger in future questions. Thus, our student here should edit her constitutional law outline by adding the facts from the missed question.

---

54. Answer (b) is incomplete because it does not address whether the compelling interest is narrowly tailored. Answer (c) is a version of the same thing as (b) with the added legalese *parens patriae* to distract the reader.

First, she should find the correct issue in the outline.

> **Issue:** Substantive due process (governmental interference with a <u>fundamental right</u>)

Now, *before the rule,* she should add a box containing the facts that triggered the issue from the question she missed.[55]

> **Issue:** Substantive due process (governmental interference with a <u>fundamental right</u>)
>
> | Looks like: | Does not look like: |
> |---|---|
> | Right to marry/procreate/raise children (identifies the fundamental right)

Example: Statute requires married parents to pay to complete a course to get divorced, and P has no money. | |

In the above example, the outline will now contain specific facts to help the student recognize the fundamental rights issue she failed to spot on the practice exam.

---

55. The facts that trigger an issue should come before the rule since you need to recognize trigger facts to spot the issue before you can apply the rule.

ERRONEOUSLY RELATING KEY FACTS TO THE WRONG ISSUE

Now let's assume that the student selected (a) as the correct answer because, while she recognized some trigger facts, she believed incorrectly that these facts required an equal protection analysis.[56] In other words, she failed to spot the correct issue *and* attributed the trigger facts to an incorrect issue.

In this situation, in addition to adding the trigger facts to the correct issue as the student did in the above example, she should also *find and correct the issue in the outline where her understanding was incorrect*. If the student believed incorrectly that this fact pattern was an equal protection question requiring strict scrutiny because married parents are a protected class, then she should add this example to that equal protection section of her outline to indicate what an equal protection issue requiring strict scrutiny does *not* look like so that she will not make this mistake on future questions. Such a correction might look like the following.

Issue: Equal protection

Looks like:	Does not look like:
	Married parents are not a protected class—Statute that only requires married parents and not married childless couples to complete a course before being able to get a divorce.

---

56. Answer (a) is wrong because merely being treated differently does not violate the equal protection clause. Furthermore, married parents are not a protected class, so only a rational basis analysis would be applicable for an equal protection argument here.

Here, the student needed to revise her outline in two places because her mistake was to attribute key facts *to the wrong issue*. Thus, in this situation you should be adding the facts as examples in two places in your outline:

1. the correct issue that you missed (as a "looks like" entry), and

2. the incorrect answer you believed was correct (as a "does not look like" entry).

SEEING AN ISSUE NOT TRIGGERED IN THE FACT PATTERN

Another common issue-spotting problem occurs when the student incorrectly believes facts in the hypothetical trigger a legal issue. Let's assume in another missed question that the same student believed incorrectly that the fundamental right to marry and raise children means children have a constitutional right to an education. Consequently, she missed another constitutional law question that contained facts about children and education.

Here, because she saw an issue that wasn't really there, she wants to add that additional fact pattern to the constitutional law outline as a "does not look like" entry.

Issue: Substantive due process (governmental interference with a <u>fundamental right</u>)

Looks like:	Does not look like:
Right to marry/procreate/raise children	Does not include a right to an education.
Example: Statute requires married parents to pay to complete a course to get divorced, and P has no money.	Example: Statute creating gifted programs in school and child's scores are too low for him to qualify.

She needs to add those facts to her outline so for the next exam, she will know that a right to an education is *not* part of the fundamental right to marry and raise children.

Again, the student does not need to include examples for all fundamental rights, only for those that she missed on practice exams.[57] This way when reviewing the outline before an exam, the student is reviewing only the factual triggers that she hasn't yet mastered. You should apply this technique not only for major issues you fail to spot, but also for any sub-issues, exceptions, or defenses that you fail to spot.

As you may remember, we listed examples of these issues and their trigger facts in Chapter 16, "Did I Misread the Fact Pattern?" In that chapter, we assumed that you knew what facts could trigger the issue but that you were missing them when reading the questions quickly. We advised you to circle the trigger facts to help you see and remember them when selecting the correct answer. If you are missing these trigger facts because you didn't understand that they triggered the issue, sub-issue, exception, or defense in the first place, however, then you also need to add the trigger facts to your outline so that you can memorize them for future questions.

TIME TO EVALUATE

Look at the questions you missed and the explanatory answers. Did you miss the issue for any of the following reasons?

1. **You failed to recognize the key facts that raised the issue.**

    Example: You failed to recognize that facts discussing marriage or divorce implicated a fundamental right.

    If yes, then make the correction on your outline by adding the key facts to the outline to show what the correct issue "looks like" on an exam.

---

57. The outline itself, however, should contain a list of the fundamental rights categories after the rule.

2. **You erroneously related key facts to the wrong issue.**

Example: You thought the question called for an equal protection analysis rather than a substantive due process analysis.

If yes, then make the correction on your outline by

a. adding the key facts to the outline to show what the correct issue "looks like" on an exam.

b. adding the key facts to the outline to show what the issue "does not look like" in a fact pattern.

3. **You erroneously believed the facts triggered an issue that was not present in the fact pattern.**

Example: You thought that the fundamental right to marry and raise children included the child's right to an education.

If yes, then make the correction on your outline by adding those facts to the outline to show what the issue "does not look like" in a fact pattern.

A FINAL NOTE ON ISSUE SPOTTING

Don't skip this step! If you cannot identify the correct *issue*, then you will not know what *rule* to apply and cannot select the correct answer. Knowing the rules is not enough. Reading the "correct answer" on a practice exam is often not enough to correct your analysis on future exams. Revising your outline will ensure you spot the correct issues on future exams.

Once you have corrected your issue-spotting problems as outlined above, or if you don't have issue-spotting problems, then the next question is whether your substantive knowledge weakness lies in your knowledge and mastery of the *rules*.

CHAPTER 19

Did I Miss the *Rule* for the Fact Pattern?

If you were able to narrow your multiple-choice answers to the correct *issue*, but you still chose the wrong answer, then you need to *make sure that you are applying the correct rule*. When you miss a question because you didn't know the correct rule, you want to ask yourself the following questions to determine where your knowledge of the rule broke down.

Common Problem with Rules

- Is the rule on my outline correct?

- Have I memorized the rule correctly?

- Is the rule on my outline complete?

Let's look at these one at a time.

IS THE RULE ON MY OUTLINE CORRECT?

If the rule on your outline is incorrect, then it won't matter how well you remember it—your resulting analysis will be flawed. Why do students' outlines contain incorrect rules? Several common scenarios lead students to define rules incorrectly in their outlines.

- Students may write down an incorrect or incomplete version of the rule. This is often a result of using the shorthand a professor uses in class for describing a rule and failing to understand that the rule entails more than the shorthand.[58]

- Besides simply misunderstanding and/or writing down an incorrect rule, students may confuse rules used by a majority of jurisdictions with rules from a minority jurisdiction and put only one rule, sometimes the minority rule, in their outlines.

- Students may also include outdated rules, particularly if a professor spent time discussing them in class. Professors can spend a lot of class time, especially in the first year, explaining the evolution of the common law and its rules. Unfortunately, for most issue-spotting exams, including multiple-choice exams, the only rules that matter are the ones that are in effect at the time you take the exam (unless your professor's multiple-choice question specifically tells you to apply some other rule).

- Perhaps the most common cause of incorrect rules in student outlines comes from using commercial outlines or outlines you've obtained from other students. When you copy, cut and paste, or simply study from another's outline, you may make critical errors that change the rules, or you may be copying rules that are incomplete, incorrect, or outdated in the first place. Furthermore, because you haven't yet mastered that material, you aren't always able to recognize the errors, so you don't realize you are memorizing bad law.[59]

---

58. For example, a torts professor may refer to "intent" in teaching battery, an intentional tort, to his class. What he really means is "an intent to cause a harmful or offensive contact or to act with knowledge that a harmful or offensive contact is substantial certainty to occur." Rather than repeat the rule fully each time, the professor assumes the student can read the full rule in the case and simply refers to the element as "intent."

59. This is why we *strongly* urge you to create your own outlines; much of the necessary memorization and understanding of the rules comes from synthesizing and writing down the material for yourself. Use these other outlines only as a backup reference to check whether your outline is correct and complete—don't use them as a starting point.

Don't rely on others to provide the correct rules for you—always think critically and check the rules that you include in your outline. Sources to check for correct rules are professors, cases, peers, and commercial outlines, in that order. But always keep in mind the reliability of the source. If you are taking a law school exam, rely first on your professor. If you are taking the bar exam, rely first on your bar review materials.

For an example of where an incorrect rule may cause you to choose the wrong answer, let's look at the following multiple-choice question in your property class.

Owen and James were business partners who owned Happy Orchards as tenants in common. Five years ago, James died and left "all of my estate" to Scott, his son, in his valid will. Owen continued to harvest Happy Orchards after James' death, earning $50,000 a year in profits from the orchards. Owen has refused to give Scott any of the profits Owen has earned from Happy Orchards in the past five years. Scott has decided to sue Owen for half of the profits.

If Scott loses his case, it will be because

a. Scott has only a future interest in Happy Orchards, so he is not entitled to past profits.
b. Owen has the right to possess the entire property and to retain the profits resulting from the use of the property.
c. Happy Orchards was not part of James' estate since Owen had the right of survivorship.
d. Scott's interest in Happy Orchards will ripen only upon Owen's death.

These answer choices all depend on understanding what a tenancy-in-common is—in other words, the answers are all concerned with rules defining how a tenancy-in-common works. Here, if you chose answer (c), an incorrect answer, instead of (b), the correct answer, you should then *look at the answer explanation to see why the answer you selected was wrong.* Answer (c) is incorrect because a tenancy-in-common is a concurrent estate without any right of survivorship, but answer (c) states that a tenancy-in-common does have the right of survivorship.

Now you need to figure out why you chose the wrong rule. Look at your property outline and see what rule it gives for defining a tenancy in common. If it says:

Issue: Tenancy-in-common

Rule: Concurrent estate where two or more parties possess the property simultaneously with right of survivorship.

Then you know the problem is that you have studied and memorized an incorrect statement of the rule. Change the rule in your outline, highlight the changes, and rememorize the correct version of the rule so that it looks like this. (We use shading instead of the colored highlighting you will use in your outlines.)

Issue: Tenancy-in-common

Rule: Concurrent estate where two or more parties possess the property simultaneously WITHOUT right of survivorship.

You highlight the changes you made to your outline because it indicates that you learned this rule incorrectly. By highlighting only the changes you made, you can quickly go back and review only those rules for the next exam.

Additionally, if you missed a rule because you are mixing up the definitions with other rules in the same category, be sure those other categories have the correct rules also. For example, now that you know you wrote down the rule for tenancy-in-common incorrectly, you would want to check your rules for the other types of concurrent estates, such as joint tenancy and tenancies in the entirety, to be sure that those rules are correct.

HAVE I MEMORIZED THE RULE CORRECTLY?

Another error students make is that they have not fully memorized the rule, so the exam drafters are able to *trick or confuse them with incorrect or incomplete statements of the rule.* This problem overlaps with a misreading problem—misreading the rule in the call of the question (see Chapter 14). The difference between a misreading problem and a substantive knowledge problem is that when you have a misreading problem, you have correctly memorized the rule, but you incorrectly read the full rule into the answer choice because you are reading quickly—you supply words that aren't there. When you haven't memorized that rule to begin with, slowing down or using our system cannot correct the problem. You must go back and learn the rule.

How do you know that you need to go back and memorize rules? Let's take the tenancy-in-common example we just discussed. Let's say you missed the question and you went back to your outline. The rule in your outline is written correctly.

> **Issue:**   Tenancy-in-common
>
> **Rule:**   Concurrent estate where two or more parties possess the property simultaneously without right of survivorship.

So now you know that your problem is one of *incomplete memorization.* You don't know the rules for the different concurrent estates well enough to tell one from the other on a test, even though you wrote the overall rule down correctly in your outline. How do you correct for this?

First, go back to your outline and *highlight the rule that you missed so that it grabs your attention*. Here again, the highlight tells you, at a glance, that you have problems with this rule.

> **Issue:**   Tenancy-in-common
>
> **Rule:**   Concurrent estate where two or more parties possess the property simultaneously without right of survivorship.

Second, *write the rule on a flashcard* with the issue listed on the other side. Review the flashcards containing rules you need to memorize until you know them cold. If you have already been using flashcards to memorize rules for multiple-choice exams, eliminate the flashcards that you know by heart so that all that remains are the ones you haven't mastered. This way you can be more efficient in your daily memorization by not wasting time on rules and issues that you already know. Add colored highlighting to the flashcards if colors help you remember and visualize the contents of the card. Also, try reading your flashcards out loud as you are studying them. For some people, hearing and/or speaking the rule as they are looking at it helps reinforce the correct version of the rule in their memories so that they can pull it up quickly on a multiple-choice exam.

IS THE RULE ON MY OUTLINE COMPLETE?

Often problems with rules are not just a matter of having written them down incorrectly or having failed to memorize them adequately. Many times the problem is that students have included incomplete rules in their outlines so they are unable to answer questions that are testing the nuances of the rules. A rule on an outline can be incomplete in many ways.

Common Reasons for Incomplete Rule Statements

- Students may use shorthand and inadvertently omit key words and concepts from the rule.

- The rule may be poorly drafted so students cannot see the relationship between its parts.

- The outline may include the overall rule but fail to include rules defining elements and sub-elements of the rule.

- The outline may not contain exceptions or defenses to the rule.

Use of shorthand for the rule

The first reason, using shorthand for the rules in your outline, is often the root cause for the other three reasons students have incomplete rule statements in the outline. Obviously, the purpose of a law school outline is to distill and condense the law into a manageable size so that you can learn it efficiently. In the process, however, details necessarily need to be left out. The trick is to ensure that you are not *omitting something that you need to know to apply the law.* We all use "shorthand" to express legal rules, and that works so long as the shorthand is enough to remind you of the entire rule. If it doesn't, you need to go back to your outline for the issue and write in the longer version of the rule. For example, let's say your personal property outline contains the following rule for an inter vivos gift.

An inter vivos gift = intent, delivery, and acceptance.

If you never miss a gift question on a practice exam, this shorthand version of the rule is sufficient for you. But notice what the above version of the rule *does not* contain. It does not tell you *whose* intent[60] *to do what*, *who* must deliver the item and *to whom*, or *who* accepted the gift. The *who* is not the same for all elements; the actors here include both a donor and a donee.

Drafting a rule to show the relationship between its parts

A more complete drafting of the rule might look like this.

An inter vivos gift is complete when

1. donor intends to give donee a gift, and

2. donor delivers the gift to donee, and

3. donee accepts the gift.

Also, notice that by including the word "and" after each element, you tell yourself that all three elements are required for the gift to succeed; this tells you *the relationship between the parts.* Now this rule is much more complete.

Drafting a rule to include definitions

Next, let's say that after these revisions to the rule in your outline you still miss a gift question. When you look at the explanation for the correct answer, you realize you missed the question because you are confused about what *intent* is. From the question's answer, you realize the definition for an inter vivos gift in your outline is still omitting key ideas for the

---

60. Intent is one of those words that is used in many different areas of law. Intent cries out for further definition because it does not always have a "commonsense" meaning. For intentional torts, for example, your outline needs to be clear that intent refers to an intent to do the act—not an intent to cause the harm.

donor's intent. The intent must be *a present intent*,[61] and the donor must intend the gift to be *permanent* (a transfer of ownership, not just a transfer of possession). These ideas must now be added to the rule in your outline to be rememorized.

An inter vivos gift is complete when

1. donor has a <u>present intent</u> to permanently transfer ownership of the gift to donee, and

2. donor delivers the gift to donee, and

3. donee accepts the gift.

Now our *overall* rule for inter vivos gifts is complete.

Drafting a rule to include its elements, sub-elements, and exceptions

We may not be done with the rule section for inter vivos gifts, however. Law professors and bar exam drafters do not test only main rules; exceptions and sub-rules are favorite testing subjects for multiple-choice questions. Therefore, you want to be sure that you know any *sub-rules, sub-elements, or exceptions* that pertain to the topic. The easiest way to "know" them is to include them in your outline.

For example, let's assume here that you have a multiple-choice question where the donor intends to give jewelry to the donee, but the jewels stay in the donor's safety deposit box and the donor gives the key to the safety deposit box only to the donee. The rule section of the outline for inter vivos gifts as written above does not give us enough information to determine whether the gift is valid because a sub-rule is missing: We don't

---

61. Not an intent to give the gift in the future. For example, saying, "I will give you my ring when you get married" to someone who isn't even engaged is not a statement of present intent.

know what delivery means. For an inter vivos gift, delivery can be actual or symbolic/constructive. If you missed that multiple-choice question, you would add that sub-rule definition to your outline and highlight it so that it would look like this.

An inter vivos gift is complete when

1. donor has a <u>present intent</u> to permanently transfer ownership of the gift to donee; and

2. donor delivers the gift to the donee; and

   - Delivery can be actual or symbolic/constructive.

3. donee accepts the gift.

Multiple-choice questions often test the sub-elements of one part of the rule or exceptions to the rule, and so these must be included in your outline and memorized as well.

To see another example of how you would include sub-elements and exceptions to rules in your outline, let's look at contracts. The overall rule in contracts is that an enforceable contract requires an offer, acceptance, consideration, and no formation defenses. This might appear in your contracts outline in the following shorthand.

Enforceable K = (a) offer + (b) acceptance + (c) consideration + (d) no formation defenses.

But this rule alone is not nearly enough to answer complicated contracts questions, as any first-year law student quickly learns. The first requirement, an offer, has sub-elements that are required before there is a valid offer. These sub-elements need to be in your outline.

Enforceable K = (a) offer + (b) acceptance + (c) consideration + (d) no formation defenses.

a. Offer requires

    1. intent, *and*

    2. definite and certain terms, *and*

    3. communication to offeree.

All of these sub-rules may require definitions[62] explaining what they are, as we just did for the elements of an inter vivos gift, so that you are clear on what these sub-rules mean.

For example, a common area to test the overall concept of an offer is whether an advertisement is enough to constitute an offer. To answer that question, you must analyze all of the sub-elements of an offer—intent, definite and certain terms, and communication to offeree. Here, the word "intent" on the outline is probably not enough to remind you what the law requires to satisfy this element. Thus, if you miss multiple-choice questions on this topic, you need to go back to your outline and flesh out this sub-element with accurate sub-rules.

Enforceable K = (a) offer + (b) acceptance + (c) consideration + (d) no formation defenses.

a. Offer requires

    1. an intent to make a commitment, *and*

       • Rule re: Ads—An ad is only an invitation to customers to make an offer; it is not an intent to make a commitment. Thus, it is not an offer.

    2. with definite and certain terms, *and*

    3. communication to offeree.

---

62. And may require examples to help with your application of the sub-rules, as we will illustrate in the next chapter.

Note: Here this sub-rule is a definition of what an offer is not. Definition rules indicating *what something is not* are just as important as definition rules that say *what something is.* All sub-elements and sub-rules are fair game for testing, so you want to make sure they are all included in the outline, especially when you missed multiple-choice questions on that topic.

But we are still not done here, because we also need to include applicable exceptions: multiple-choice exams *love to test exceptions.* Here, as you covered in your contracts class, some advertisements can constitute valid offers. Advertisements that include the quantity of the item for sale and words of promise, such as "first come first served," can constitute offers. Thus, this exception to the rule needs to be included in the outline.

Enforceable K = (a) offer + (b) acceptance + (c) consideration + (d) no formation defenses.

a. Offer requires

    1. an intent to make a commitment, *and*

       • Rule re: Ads—An ad is only an invitation to customers to make an offer; it is not an intent to make a commitment. Thus, it is not an offer.

       • Exception: An ad that includes *all* the material terms *and* identifies the offeree is an offer. (Intent is reflected in the specifics of the ad.)

    2. with definite and certain terms, *and*

    3. communication to offeree.

TIME TO EVALUATE

Look at the questions you missed and the explanatory answers. Assuming you were able to correctly spot the issue, did you choose the wrong answers for any of the following reasons?

1. **The rule was missing from your outline.**

2. **The rule in your outline was not correct.**

3. **The rule in your outline was not complete.**

> If applicable, the rule should include

a. all sub-parts (or elements)

b. exceptions

c. defenses

4. **The rule was not sufficiently descriptive to enable you to apply the rule correctly to the fact pattern.**

> Descriptive means the rule should:

a. identify the actors;

b. include definitions;

c. show the relationship, if any, between the various parts of the rule.

5. **You failed to memorize the rule correctly.**

If you answered "yes" to any of the first four questions, make the corrections to your outline as described in this chapter. Remember, we are not saying you must revise *all* the rule statements in your outline, *only those you missed on practice exams.*

If you answered "yes" to question 5, use whatever technique helps you best memorize the rule (e.g., flashcards, speaking the rule, or repeatedly writing the rule). While your memorization of the rule does not need to be as "perfect" for a multiple-choice exam as it does for an essay exam, your knowledge of the rule has to be "perfect enough" to enable you to choose the correct answer. In addition to these memorization techniques, don't forget to consider your time management. You must have enough time *before* the exam to work on memorizing the rules.

A FINAL NOTE ON RULES

When preparing your substantive outline, take the time to *think* about the rules. Remember the IRAC relationship. For every issue, sub-issue, or sub-

sub-issue, a rule generally follows. Understanding the rule directs your application of that rule to the facts.

If the rule in your outline is missing, incorrect, incomplete, or simply incomprehensible to you, you will probably choose the wrong answer on a multiple-choice exam. If, however, your outlines contain all the steps we have outlined in this rules section and you are still missing multiple-choice questions because you have identified a substantive knowledge problem, then next you need to see whether your problem is with the *application* of those rules to the facts in the questions.

CHAPTER 20

Did I Miss the *Application* for the Fact Pattern?

If you have corrected for problems spotting the issue and you have ensured that you have memorized all the correct rules but you are still missing multiple-choice questions because of a substantive knowledge problem, then you are having issues with the application step of the analysis. In other words, you can recognize the issues raised by a fact pattern and you are able to recite the applicable rules in detail, but you still failed to choose the right answer. The problem—you don't know *how to apply the rules to the facts to answer the call of the question*. Being able to apply rules to facts correctly is one of the most fundamental skills a lawyer has. Improving your skills in this area will not only make you a better law school and bar exam test taker, it will pave the way for success in your future law practice.

In general, students have several types of problems when it comes to the application step of the analysis.

Common Application Problems

- Students don't understand the factual context in which a given rule operates, and so they are unable to recognize the significance of key facts in the multiple-choice questions that determine the correct answer.

- Students don't understand how a rule's elements operate in relation to other elements.

- Students don't understand how to analyze questions that require value judgments. (These are the questions that ask for the "best" answer when several answers are true.)

UNDERSTANDING THE RULE'S FACTUAL CONTEXT

The first type of application problem, not understanding how the rule operates with specific facts, often appears to be a misreading problem: The student misses key facts in the question and so she chooses the wrong answer. When the student has only a misreading problem, the student knows the facts are significant, but she simply forgets them or doesn't see them when reading a long and complex fact pattern. In contrast, with a substantive problem, the student misses the significant facts because she doesn't understand what facts are key to the analysis.

Correcting this kind of substantive problem requires *adding factual examples with legal reasoning* to your outline in much the same way that you added facts to your outline to improve your issue-spotting ability. This time, you would add the key facts and their legal significance (the reasoning) *after* the rule. You want to keep the facts in IRAC order. The facts that trigger the issue are not the same as the facts that belong in the outline's application section. The facts that trigger the rule only *raise* the issue—what the issue looks like or doesn't look like. These facts don't tell you how to determine whether the issue *is or is not satisfied*. The facts in the application section should be factual examples and reasoning showing how the issue was resolved based on prior cases or class hypotheticals.

Once you've identified the key facts and the reasoning (e.g., why they are significant to the analysis),[63] you should add them to your outline and memorize them just as you memorized trigger facts to help you issue-spot. You use these examples as the basis for your application of the rule. To see how we would do this, take a look at the following fact pattern.

Understanding key facts in general

Pat was playing softball in the park when he saw Tony walking down the street. Pat was angry at Tony because that morning Tony had parked in Pat's parking space and Pat had to park three blocks away. Pat took the softball and threw it hard at Tony's head. The softball missed Tony by several yards and smashed into a car window behind Tony, who whipped around to look at the car window after the impact.

   Under these facts, Pat is liable to Tony for

a. battery.
b. assault.
c. both battery and assault.
d. neither battery nor assault.

Here, the correct answer is (d) ("neither battery nor assault"). Let's assume for the moment that our student chose the incorrect answer, (b) ("assault"). The student knows that the correct rule for assault is

---

63. To be found in the explanations for the correct answer choices.

> Assault is an intentional act by defendant that creates a reasonable apprehension of an imminent harmful or offensive contact in plaintiff.

because that is the rule in his torts outline that he memorized. Although the student knew the rule cold, upon talking to the student, we realized that he did not understand how the part of the rule stating "reasonable apprehension of an imminent harmful . . . contact" would look factually. This is why he did not recognize that the words "Tony . . . whipped around . . . after the impact," were facts indicating Tony never felt any apprehension. Tony didn't anticipate being hit because he didn't know Pat threw the ball until after it hit the car (when it was no longer a threat to Tony). Because the student didn't understand how to apply this part of the rule, he failed to see the significance of these facts and couldn't determine that the assault rule was not satisfied here.

When you miss a question because you don't know how to apply a rule or an element of a rule, you want to add those key application facts and the reason why they are legally significant to your outline as an example so that you will remember how to apply the rule to similar facts in future questions. Thus, our student from the example above should edit his outline below the rule to add in facts and reasoning from the question he missed as follows.

> **Issue:** Assault
>
> **Rule:** An intentional act by defendant that creates a reasonable apprehension of an imminent harmful or offensive contact in plaintiff.
>
> | Is: | Is not: |
> |---|---|
> | Apprehension of imminent harm | No apprehension of imminent harm: When D throws a ball at P's head but P doesn't even know D threw it until it misses P and hits a window. No apprehension because P didn't see it coming. |

This student's outline now contains a specific application of the rule to facts to help the student learn to apply that rule correctly. Now he knows which facts *do not* satisfy the assault rule and *why* (the reasoning). If the student is still unsure when the rule is satisfied, the student should add an example of facts and reasoning that *do* satisfy the assault rule. Using additional assault hypotheticals from cases and class notes, the student should fill in facts that satisfy the apprehension of imminent harm element so that his outline now looks like this.

Issue: Assault

Rule: An intentional act by defendant that creates a reasonable apprehension of an imminent harmful or offensive contact in plaintiff.

Is:	Is not:
Apprehension of imminent harm:	No apprehension of imminent harm:
When P sees D swing a hammer at P's hand and P tries to pull his hand out of the way to avoid injury.	When D throws a ball at P's head but P doesn't even know D threw it until it misses P and hits a window. No apprehension because P didn't see it coming.

When the student reviews this outline, he now has examples of how to apply the assault rule to specific kinds of facts and the resulting conclusion of that application. The student should add additional examples if he continues to struggle with the concept of apprehension of imminent harm.

If apprehension of imminent harm was the only element of assault that the student was unable to analyze successfully, then he would be finished revising the assault section of his outline. But if that student went on to find he was struggling to understand how other elements of the assault rule should be applied as he took practice tests, he would add these in to his outline after the rule as well. Here, for example, are application examples for some other elements of the assault rule.

Is/Looks like:	Is not/Does not look like:
Is an <u>intentional act</u>: When D throws a rock at the P while looking right at P.	Not an <u>intentional act</u>: When D kicks a ball without aiming at P.
Is <u>apprehension of imminent harm</u>: When P sees D swing a hammer at P's hand and P tries to pull his hand out of the way to avoid injury.	No <u>apprehension of imminent harm</u>: When D throws a ball at P's head but P doesn't even know D threw it until it misses P and hits a window. No apprehension because P didn't see it coming.
Is <u>harmful or offensive</u>: When D throws a hammer at P because a hammer can hurt.	Not <u>harmful or offensive</u>: When D throws a piece of popcorn at P because popcorn doesn't hurt and isn't insulting.

Understanding key facts to differentiate between closely related legal issues

Another example of where failing to understand the key facts results in choosing an incorrect answer is when the answer choice contains two closely related legal issues.

Example 1

Take a look at the following contracts fact pattern.

Paula inherited a desk from her grandfather that Paula's mother told her was an excellent twentieth-century copy of a seventeenth-century French writing desk. Paula had no room for the desk and decided to sell it. She placed an ad with a photo of the desk offering to sell "a twentieth-century replica French writing desk" for $1000. Debra, a French antiques dealer who sells copies and originals in her store, saw the ad online. Debra e-mailed Paula saying she wanted to buy the desk. Paula e-mailed Debra her agreement, and Debra picked up the desk the next day. A week later Paula was walking by Debra's shop when she saw her writing desk for sale in the window with a sign saying, "seventeenth-century French writing desk, $10,000."

Assuming that the desk is an authentic seventeenth-century French writing desk, Paula's best argument to void the contract and get the desk back is

a. Statute of Frauds.
b. mutual mistake of fact.
c. unilateral mistake of fact.
d. mutual mistake of law.

Let's assume that the student realized the contracts issue here was whether the contract was voidable because of a material mistake of fact.[64] However, she incorrectly chose answer (c), unilateral mistake, when the correct answer is (b), mutual mistake. She could have made this error because of either a rule error *or* an application error.

A *rule error* exists if the student did not know that with mistake rules, the focus is on what the parties knew at the time the contract was made. If that was the reason for choosing the wrong answer, then she needs to add a note to her outline on *both* the issues of unilateral and mutual mistake to focus on the time the contract was made. However, if the student correctly stated the mistake rules—focusing on what the parties knew at the time of

---

64. The Statute of Frauds does not apply because the contract was in writing—the terms were in the ad and in the subsequent e-mails. The mistake is not one of law because it involves the authenticity of the desk, a factual matter.

the contract—then the error lies in her knowledge of the key facts in applying the rules. (Remember, *always* check for a rule error before an application one.)

An *application error* exists if she focused on what the parties knew at the time the contract was entered into but thought that because Debra was an antiques dealer, she knew the desk was authentic. This would lead this student to select (c) rather than (b). Here, however, the key facts are that even though Debra was an antiques dealer, she had no basis for knowing the desk was not a replica because she had never seen the actual desk, only a picture of it, when she agreed to buy it. Both the seller and the buyer thought the desk was a replica *at the time of the contract.*

Understanding this error in her original analysis, the student should take her contracts outline and correct it in two ways. First, she should add the following to the section on unilateral mistake.

Issue:	Unilateral mistake of fact

Rule: No rescission of the contract for the mistaken party unless the mistake was material and the other party knew or should have known of the mistake at the time the contract was made.

Is:	Is not:
	No unilateral mistake:
	When seller sells desk she believes is a copy and not an antique to antiques dealer *who never saw the actual desk (only a photo) until after the sale was complete.* Antiques dealer did not know or have reason to know the desk was real at the time of the sale.

Second, the student should then turn to the mutual mistake part of her contracts outline and add the key facts and reasoning from the hypothetical she missed.

Issue: Mutual mistake of fact

Rule: Rescission or reformation of a contract is available when both parties, at the time the contract was made, are mistaken about a fact material to the contract.

Is:	Is not:
Mutual mistake:	
When seller sells desk she believes is a copy and not an antique to antiques dealer *who never saw the actual desk (only a photo) until after the sale was complete.* At time of the sale both parties believed incorrectly that the desk was a replica.	

Adding this question's facts and reasoning to *both* the unilateral mistake section and to the mutual mistake section of the outline will ensure that the student will not confuse the key facts on these two issues on similar multiple-choice questions in the future.

Example 2

Here is another example of where failing to understand the key facts leads to choosing the wrong answer. This criminal law question involves looking at two concepts that sound similar but are actually separate concepts: general versus specific intent.[65] Both concepts are concerned about the defendant's intent (hence the confusion), but the concepts require looking at *different facts* about the defendant's intent.

For general intent crimes, the intent question is whether the defendant intended to commit the act. For example, the crime of battery requires general intent: The defendant must intend harmful physical contact—it cannot be a mere accident. In contrast, for specific intent crimes, the defendant must intend not only the act, but also the specific crime or its consequences. For example, for the specific intent crime of larceny, the defendant must not only wrongfully intend to take the property, the defendant must also intend to deprive the owner of the property permanently.

If a student has difficulty applying intent rules, this can mean either a rule error *or* an application error. It is a *rule error* if the outline fails to identify which crimes require specific intent. To correct this rule error, the student must edit the outline to add, for each crime, whether the crime is a general intent crime *or* a specific intent crime.

It is an *application error* if the rule does specify which form of intent is needed but despite the clear rule, the student is unable to identify the key facts that apply to the rule. To correct this application error, the student must edit the outline to add the key facts and the reasons why that intent (whether general or specific) is or is not satisfied.

For example, suppose the student keeps missing questions like the following about the crime of larceny.

---

65. The concept of intent is particularly confusing because the word "intent" appears as elements in both criminal and tort law, but the concepts are not the same. The standard for specific intent crimes, acting with a specific purpose to cause a harm, is usually a more restrictive definition than the intent required for intentional torts, which includes acting while "knowing with substantial certainty" that a harm will occur.

Jason, a college student, went to a card game and proceeded to lose $3000 to Bill, a professional gambler. Bill told Jason that he needed the money right away because Bill owed Greg $6000. Jason did not have enough money with him to pay his debt to Bill, so Jason went back to his dorm room and took his roommate Dan's gold watch, which Dan had told Jason was worth $6000. Dan never wore the watch and kept it in an unlocked box on his dresser.

Jason handed the watch to Bill and told Bill he had borrowed the watch from Dan. He asked Bill to hold on to the watch as collateral until Jason was able to go home that coming weekend and get cash for Bill. Bill agreed. Unfortunately, Dan noticed the watch was missing the next day and called the police. When questioned by police, Jason admitted he had given Dan's watch to Bill. When the police questioned Bill, Bill told them he had given the watch to Greg.

Which of the following statements is true?

a. Jason is guilty of larceny.
b. Jason is guilty of burglary.[66]
c. Jason is guilty of burglary and larceny.
d. Jason is guilty of neither burglary nor larceny.

Assuming the larceny rule was correctly stated in this student's outline but the student incorrectly chose (a), the student made an application error, not a rule error. Answer (a) is incorrect because although the general intent requirement is satisfied—Jason did intentionally and wrongfully take Dan's watch—the *specific intent requirement was not.* Jason had no intent to permanently deprive Dave of his watch because Jason believed he would get the watch back to return to Dan.

To correct this application error, the student then needs to edit his larceny outline as follows.

---

66. Burglary is a red herring here since Jason did not break or enter into the dwelling. As Dan's roommate, Jason had every right to be there.

Issue: Larceny

Rule:

1. Wrongful taking of another's property *and*

2. Intent to deprive owner of it permanently—*specific intent required*

Application:

1. Wrongful taking

Is (a wrongful taking):	Is not (a wrongful taking):
A takes his roommate's watch to give to C as collateral without the roommate's knowledge.	B loans A, his roommate, B's watch to use as collateral for a loan.

2. Specific intent to deprive permanently

Is (specific intent):	Is not (specific intent):
A is angry at B and takes B's watch and throws it in the ocean where it is swept out to sea.	A takes B's watch and gives it to C as collateral until A can pay C and get the watch to return it to B (no intent to deprive B permanently).

Adding clear notations to the outline indicating when a crime[67] is a specific intent crime and giving clear examples of when that specific intent is and is not satisfied will help students answer multiple-choice questions involving the concept of intent correctly.

---

67. If a student misses torts questions regarding intent for intentional torts, the student should illustrate the applicable intent requirement with an "Intent is/Intent is not" box just like the illustration here for the specific intent crime of larceny.

Understanding key facts for broad and nonspecific rules

Another type of rule where almost all students would benefit from adding clear examples containing facts and holdings to their outlines are rules with broad and nonspecific language. Rules containing words such as *foreseeability, reasonableness,* or *totality of the circumstances* are difficult to apply correctly. A student may have no difficulty spotting the issue and recalling the rule, but may have no clear idea what is "reasonable" or "foreseeable" without adding specific examples showing how that rule operates to the outline.

So, for example, in the negligence section of your torts outline, after your negligence rule stating

Issue: Duty

Rule: Defendant owes a duty to a foreseeable plaintiff within the zone of danger.

you would add examples to help define the parameters of foreseeability in your mind.

Is:	Is not:
Foreseeable P:	Not a foreseeable P:
When driver hits pedestrian Adam in crosswalk because driver was texting and not looking. Adam was a foreseeable P.	When driver hits a car with a bomb inside that explodes. John, five blocks away, is injured when a clock falls off the wall because of the vibrations from the explosion and hits John on the head. John was not a foreseeable P.

Remember, for multiple-choice questions the answer must be "yes" or "no" and not "maybe," so factual examples of "reasonableness" or "foreseeability" or "totality of the circumstances" will become easier for you to apply if you know exactly how similar key facts have been applied in the past.

UNDERSTANDING HOW THE RULES OPERATE

In Chapter 16, we discuss the importance of having the correct and complete rules in your outline. As we explained, you want your rules to state clearly how the sub-elements relate to one another. Are the sub-rules alternatives, requirements, or factors?[68] If they are requirements, are the elements dependent or independent requirements? Failure to understand these relationships and their significance can lead to confusion when applying these rules on a multiple-choice exam, causing you to select the wrong answer.

Alternatives, requirements, or factors?

A rule can be written in a variety of ways.

1. **In the alternative**
   Example: Intent for the tort of battery is the intent to cause a harmful or offensive contact *or* to act with knowledge that a harmful or offensive contact is substantially certain to occur.

2. **As a requirement**
   Example: Common law burglary *must* take place at night.

---

68. Factors are difficult to test in multiple-choice questions because they are often balancing tests and so are better suited to essay exams. Nonetheless, carefully drafted questions may still test the application of factor or balancing tests on multiple-choice exams.

3. As factors

Example: To determine whether the defendant's conduct is extreme and outrageous for purposes of intentional infliction of emotional distress, consider the duration and intensity of the defendant's conduct, whether the defendant abused a position of power or authority over the plaintiff, whether the defendant knew about the plaintiff's susceptibility to distress, and whether the defendant's objective was legitimate.

Problems arise when the sub-elements of a rule in your outline are alternatives or factors, but you apply them as if they are requirements (or vice versa). Take a look at the following torts question.

Bob was angry at his friend Jim because Jim kept playing practical jokes on him and Jim did not stop even after Bob asked him to. To teach Jim a lesson, Bob called Jim at home one night and told Jim that there had been a terrible accident and that Jim's wife Karen had been killed. In reality, Karen was out having dinner with Bob's wife June. When Bob heard the news, he dropped the phone in shock and began to have a heart attack. Jim eventually recovered fully from the heart attack.

Bob felt terrible about Jim's heart attack. He did not know that Jim had a heart condition, and he only wanted to show Jim that practical jokes weren't funny.

Jim sues Bob for intentional infliction of emotional distress. Mostly likely Jim will

a. not prevail, because Bob did not know about Jim's heart condition and Bob was not in a position of power or authority over Jim.
b. not prevail, because Bob did not intend to cause Jim extreme emotional distress.
c. prevail, because telling Jim his wife was dead when she was not was extreme and outrageous.
d. not prevail, because Jim was just kidding.

The correct answer is (c), but let's assume the student incorrectly chose (a). Here again, the reason the student chose the wrong answer may be either a rule error *or* an application error.

A *rule error* exists if the student did not know that the rule for extreme and outrageous conduct contained factors, not requirements. If that was the reason for choosing the wrong answer, then he needs to add a note to his outline that not every factor must be met to find the defendant's conduct extreme and outrageous. (Remember, *always* check for a rule error before an application error.)

An *application error* exists if he knew that not all the factors must be met, but selected the wrong answer nevertheless. In that case, the factual example along with the reasoning has to be added to this student's outline.

Let's look at this student's torts outline on intentional infliction of emotional distress.

Issue: Intentional infliction of emotional distress

Rule (prima facie case):

1. extreme and outrageous conduct by defendant, *and*

    a. Abuse of a position of power or authority over plaintiff

    b. Knowledge of plaintiff's susceptibility to distress

    c. Intensity and duration of defendant's conduct

    d. Legitimacy of defendant's objective

2. intent to cause plaintiff's distress, *and*

3. severe emotional distress suffered by plaintiff

    a. Intensity and duration of distress

    b. Evidence of physical distress

This outline indicates a *rule error*. The rules listed under the first element, extreme and outrageous conduct, *are only factors*. None of them are required to be present for the first element to be satisfied—they are only things to look for to help the court make a decision. If the student here did not know this, he might believe that since the conduct was just one statement (not of long duration or a repeated course of conduct), since Bob did not know about Jim's vulnerability to a heart attack, and since he had no power over Jim, the extreme and outrageous element was not satisfied, even though Bob had no legitimate objective when telling Jim his wife was dead. That would lead this student to choose the incorrect answer, (a). To correct this error, this student would revise his outline to reflect factors, not requirements.

An example of an outline correction for the rule section for this element would look like this.

> 1. extreme and outrageous conduct by defendant
>   When evaluating, consider the following factors:
>
>   **a.** Abuse of a position of power or authority over plaintiff
>
>   **b.** Knowledge of P's susceptibility to distress
>
>   **c.** Intensity and duration of defendant's conduct
>
>   **d.** Legitimacy of defendant's objective
>
> **Note:** These are factors—<u>none</u> are required, but all should be considered[69] and must be balanced together.

However, the error is an *application error* if the student knew that these are only factors but selected the wrong answer anyway. To correct this error, the student needs to include factual examples on his outline of this conduct and conduct courts have determined to be extreme and outrageous (from case law and class hypotheticals) that did not satisfy all of the factors.

---

69. In fact, while (a), (b), and (c) make it *more* likely that a defendant's conduct is extreme and outrageous, factor (d) makes it *less* likely that the conduct is extreme and outrageous.

An example of an outline correction for the application section for this element would look like this.

Is extreme and outrageous:	Is not extreme and outrageous:
When defendant trash collectors association threatened plaintiff (beat him up, cut truck tires, or burn his truck) to coerce him to join the association.	Defendant store clerk telling a customer, "You stink to me," is not E&O because IIED does not guard against slights and insults.
Note: no knowledge P was susceptible to distress-other factors satisfied.	*Slocum v. Food Fair Stores of Fla.*
State Rubbish Collectors Ass'n v. Siliznoff	**Note:** No factors here.
When defendant friend tells another friend his wife died in an auto accident when the wife was actually fine.	
Note: Only two factors present: no legitimate objective, intensity of the conduct.	

Similarly, with the second element of intentional infliction of emotional distress—intent to cause plaintiff's distress—this student may choose the wrong answer on a multiple-choice exam because of either a rule error *or* an application error. The outline indicates a *rule error* if the student doesn't understand that "intent to cause" really means

1. actual intent to cause severe emotional distress, *or*

2. acting with reckless disregard for the possibility that the plaintiff would suffer severe distress.

In other words, the student must understand that "intent to cause" is really shorthand for two *alternatives*—intent to cause severe emotional distress *or* to act with reckless disregard for the possibility that the plaintiff would suffer severe distress. Only one of these is required to satisfy this element. To correct this rule error, the student would add the complete rule, highlighting the "or" to show the rule is in the alternative, to his outline.

An example of an outline correction for the rule section for this element would look like this.

2. Intent to cause plaintiff's distress
   Rule: Defendant must

   a. have the intent to cause severe emotional distress, or

   b. act with reckless disregard for the possibility that the plaintiff would suffer severe distress.

However, the error is an *application error* if the student knew these subrules *and* that these rules are alternatives but selected the wrong answer anyway. To correct this error, the student needs to include factual examples with the reasoning on his outline for both types of intent. Again, the factual examples would come from case law, class hypotheticals, and practice multiple-choice problems. In areas where the student is unable to find a factual example for a particular type of intent, such as intent to cause severe emotional distress, that "outline hole" should be noted on the outline. The student should fill that hole with a factual example before the exam by asking the professor or looking at supplemental materials. If an outline hole is not filled before the exam, the student runs the risk of being unable to analyze the facts on the exam.

An example of an outline correction for the application section would look like this.

Is intent:	Is not intent:
Intent to cause SED: When defendant told the plaintiff "I'm going to make your life so miserable that you will have to quit your job." Reckless disregard: When defendant tells plaintiff his wife died in an auto accident when plaintiff's wife was actually fine. Conduct is reckless, even though defendant didn't intend to cause his friend's heart attack but only wanted to teach him a lesson.	No intent or reckless disregard to cause SED: When defendant accidentally breaks the urn where plaintiff keeps his mother's ashes.

By studying and memorizing this revised version of the intent-to-inflict-emotional-distress outline, this student is more likely to avoid making the same mistakes on the next multiple-choice exam.

Dependent versus independent?

Even when students understand that a rule's sub-elements are requirements, they may still fail to understand whether the elements of a rule operate independently or dependently of each other. Many students analyze questions as if the elements are always independent. When elements are dependent, however, students have trouble choosing the right answer because all of the answers appear to be correct, and they don't know how to choose the "best answer" among the correct answers.

What do we mean by independent versus dependent elements? Well, let's first look at rules that have independent elements. For example, the merchant's defense to false imprisonment has three *independent elements*.

> **Merchant's Defense to False Imprisonment**
>
> 1. The merchant must have probable cause to detain the plaintiff, *and*
>
> 2. The merchant must detain the plaintiff in a reasonable manner, *and*
>
> 3. The merchant must detain the plaintiff for a reasonable time.

While all three of these elements are required for the defense to succeed, none of these elements need to be addressed in any particular order. In other words, none of them *depend* on the other. In contrast, when elements are *dependent*, there is always a threshold question and a specific order to the analysis. This means that if the answer to that threshold question is "no," *the next elements are no longer relevant.* If the answer to the threshold question is "yes," the elements that follow are relevant but still must be addressed in a specific order.

What rules have *dependent elements*? Two of the most common rules that have dependent elements are the rule for contract formation in contracts and the rule for negligence in torts. Let's look at the contracts example first.

> To form a contract requires
>
> 1. offer, *and*
>
> 2. acceptance, *and*
>
> 3. consideration.

Here, however, with no offer, *there can be no acceptance.* A buyer cannot accept an offer that has never been made. This is why the element of acceptance is *dependent* on the offer element. (In contrast, a merchant could detain a plaintiff for a reasonable time and in a reasonable manner, even though the merchant did not have probable cause to do so.)

Similarly, the elements of negligence are *dependent* on each other.

To prove negligence, a plaintiff must prove

1. defendant owed a duty of care to plaintiff, *and*

2. defendant breached that duty, *and*

3. defendant's breach caused plaintiff's injury, *and*

4. defendant's breach resulted in plaintiff's damages.

Here, if the defendant did not owe the plaintiff a duty of care, none of the rest of the elements matter. A defendant cannot breach a duty if no duty exists. But if the defendant owed a duty to the plaintiff, the next issue has to be whether the duty was breached. Therefore, all the other elements are *dependent* on the threshold question—whether the defendant owed the plaintiff a duty of care. If yes, issues must be addressed in a specific order— breach, actual cause, proximate cause, and finally, damages. What does this mean in a multiple-choice question's analysis?

Let's look at the following negligence facts.

Sherry was driving her car down an empty country road on a cold and stormy night. While stopped at a stop sign, Sherry noticed Felix lying in a ditch near the road. Sherry got out of her car and walked over to Felix. When she bent over Felix to see whether he was breathing, she smelled a strong odor of alcohol on his breath. She yelled at him to wake up, but he did not respond. By this time Sherry was soaked through and shivering, so she got in her car and drove straight home and went to sleep without telling anyone about Felix. Several hours later, Jerry fell asleep at the wheel of his car on the same road. He veered off the road and hit and injured Felix, who was still lying where Sherry had left him.

> What is Sherry's best defense to a negligence claim against her by Felix?
>
> a. Sherry is not liable because Jerry was the cause in fact of Felix's injuries.
> b. Sherry is not liable because but for Felix's voluntary intoxication, Felix would not have been injured.
> c. Sherry is not liable because she acted with reasonable care when she approached Felix.
> d. Sherry is not liable because she assumed no duty to help Felix.

Here, even if answers (a), (b), and (c) contain true and correct statements of the law, (d) is still the best answer. In other words, even if there were *many reasons why this claim might fail,* (d) is still the *best* answer because not only is it a correct legal answer, it is the *threshold element* of the cause of action. If Sherry had no duty, none of the other elements come into play.

The point to remember is—whenever you have a multiple-choice question that calls for the application of a rule with dependent elements, *be sure to analyze whether the threshold element is satisfied first* before choosing an answer based on the remaining dependent elements. If the threshold element is satisfied, *then* examine the other elements in the specific order provided by the rule.

UNDERSTANDING VALUE JUDGMENTS

Many students struggle with questions that ask for the *best* answer because they don't really understand what it is these questions are asking them to decide. When the call of the question asks

- What is X's *best (or weakest)* argument? or

- Which argument is *most likely (or least likely)* to succeed?

the drafters of the question are asking you to make a *relative* judgment between the choices. What makes these questions hard for students to answer is that several of the stated answers may be true, but one of the answers *is preferable under the circumstances*, and students don't understand how to choose between them. These kinds of questions require you to know the kinds of hierarchies of choice that often come up in legal questions. These include the following.

Hierarchy of Choices

- A preference for procedural arguments over substantive arguments

- A preference for legal arguments over equitable arguments

- A preference for arguments about a prima facie case before arguments about defenses

- Preferences within particular subjects for certain types of policies or claims over others

---

Understanding how these preferences operate and recognizing when they come into play[70] will make complicated multiple-choice analyses easier and faster to navigate. Let's look briefly at each of these preferences.

Procedural over substantive arguments

Judges always consider procedural arguments *before* looking at the substance of the claims. They do this because if the case has a procedural defect, the court will reject the case on that basis and never reach the substantive arguments of the case. Thus, if a party can end a case at the procedural stage, it is a "better" argument because it will prevent the court from ever reaching the substantive questions.

---

70. You may notice that the order preferences described here is the same one your legal writing professor told you to use when writing persuasive briefs for court. The preferences determine which arguments you would put first in your legal briefs to a court.

What are some of the procedural issues that can trump a substantive answer because the court will never reach the substantive claim?

Procedural Issues That Trump Substantive Issues

- If a plaintiff lacks standing to bring a lawsuit

- If a plaintiff files a claim after the statute of limitations has passed

- If a court does not have jurisdiction

- If a controversy is not yet ripe

- If a controversy is moot

On multiple-choice "best answer" questions, this means when you have two correct answers, you would choose the correct procedural argument *before* the correct substantive one.

Legal over equitable arguments

Because a court always considers legal arguments before equitable ones, you must first analyze the fact pattern to consider legal issues before equitable ones. For example, in an action for breach of contract, a court will consider the equitable remedy of specific performance only if the moving party can prove the legal remedy of monetary damages is inadequate. Therefore, the law has created a hierarchy or order of preference to the arguments, making one argument "better" than another.

On multiple-choice questions, this means when you have two correct answers, you would choose the correct legal argument *before* the correct equitable one. Other examples follow.

Examples of Legal over Equitable Preferences

- In a contract formation question, you would argue consideration before promissory estoppel.

- In a remedies question, you would make arguments for monetary damages (legal remedy) before arguments for unjust enrichment (equitable remedy).

- In a property question, you would make arguments for damages (making the defendant pay something for injuring your property) before making arguments for an injunction (requiring the defendant to do something or refrain from doing something to your property).

Argue the prima facie case before defenses

If a correct answer choice states that the facts don't establish the prima facie case, this is a "better" option than a correct answer choice regarding a successful defense argument because procedurally the case could end with a motion to dismiss for failure to state a claim. This makes such an argument strategically "better" for the client bringing the motion and "better" for the court because the court will spend less time and resources resolving the dispute.

For example, it would be better for a defendant to show the plaintiff had no claim for false imprisonment than for the defendant to raise the merchant's defense to the false imprisonment claim. Similarly, it is better for a defendant to show that the state failed to prove the defendant trespassed than to prove that his trespass was justified by necessity or duress.

On multiple-choice questions, this means that when you have two correct answers, you would choose the correct legal argument about the prima facie case *before* the correct argument about a defense to the prima facie case.

Preferences based on policies or legal outcomes

Within certain subjects, there can be particular *policies* that make one correct answer preferable over another.

Examples of Policy Preferences

- In contracts, contractual terms are construed against the drafter.

- In property, the law prefers the free alienability of property.

Policy preferences means that between two seemingly "correct" answers, one answer may be "better" because it furthers a policy. Each area of law has its own policies and preferences that should be included in your outline.

Similarly, within individual subjects areas of law, some claims or causes of action are "better" than others because they provide a better outcome for the moving party.[71] Keep in mind that what is a "better outcome" always depends on the party's goals.

Examples of Claim Preferences

- In torts, an intentional tort claim is better for the plaintiff than a negligence claim because the plaintiff can claim punitive damages.

- In constitutional law, a substantive due process claim may be better than an equal protection claim because a substantive due process claim means that the government must stop its action versus only acting in a way that does not discriminate.

---

71. Note that for all these scenarios drafters can frame a multiple-choice question so that you would have to answer what is better for the *other* party (e.g., a finding of negligence would be better for a defendant than an intentional tort).

- In criminal law, a charge of first-degree murder is often better for the state than a manslaughter charge because the sentence is longer.

- In property, an adverse possession claim is better than a prescriptive easement claim because adverse possession gives the possessor ownership of the property instead of just the right to use the property.

Claim preferences mean that between two seemingly "correct" answers, one answer may be "better" because it furthers a particular goal—for example, more damages or more jail time. As with policy preferences, each area of law has its own claim preferences that should be included in your outline.

TIME TO EVALUATE

Look at the questions you missed and the explanatory answers. Assuming you were able to spot the issue correctly and your rule was correct, complete, and accurately memorized, did you choose the wrong answers for any of the following reasons?

1. **You were unable to recognize the *key facts* in the fact pattern that directed you to the correct answer.**

   If yes, then add examples and reasoning (key facts + reasons for the holding) to your outline for issues where you don't know how to apply the rule.

   If you saw the key facts but related those facts to the wrong issue, be sure to make the correction in two places on your outline—on the correct issue and on the incorrect one.

2. **You didn't understand how a rule's elements operate in relation to other elements making one correct answer better than another.**

   If yes, revise your outlines so that your rule statements correctly reflect whether the rules are alternatives, requirements, or factors.

   If yes, revise your outlines so the rules reflect whether they are dependent or independent of each other.

3. **You didn't understand the value judgments that made one correct answer better than another.**

If yes, revise your outlines to include the hierarchy of choices:

a. procedural over substantive arguments,

b. legal over equitable arguments,

c. prima facie case before defenses,

d. preferences for certain policies or claims over others.

The key to correcting any of these application errors is to learn from them. Read the explanatory answer and record your understanding on your outline. Remember, we are not saying you must revise *all* the application sections on your outline, *only those you missed on practice exams.*

A FINAL NOTE ON APPLICATION

Law school multiple-choice questions are generally not questions of recognition but questions of *analysis*. This kind of analysis requires you to understand not only individual rules and their application but also the relationships between different types of claims and arguments. Just as with an essay exam, you need to be aware of

1. which claims are most preferred and why,

2. which claims are preferred next,

3. what the elements of the claims are and how they are related to one another,

4. which potential defenses or exceptions apply, and

5. what policies are important for that body of law.

In legal analysis, rules and their application to facts are intertwined. Generally, the rules point you to the key facts and direct your analysis of those facts. For example, larceny's specific intent is the intent to permanently deprive another of his property. That rule statement tells you what type of facts to look for in the fact pattern and how to analyze the facts you find. Thus, if you chose the wrong answer (conclusion), then first consider your issue spotting, then examine your rule, and finally, look at your application of the rule to the facts. Always remember, *IRAC governs legal analysis.*

Caveat: This system was designed based on the premise that you would take a practice multiple-choice exam and then diagnose, evaluate, and correct your outline based on the questions you answered incorrectly. If you find you don't have time to take practice multiple-choice exams, then consider preparing a more complete outline as we have delineated in this chapter.

CHAPTER 21

Marking and Using Revised Outlines

Don't skip this part of the book!

We know: You want to. It looks difficult, it feels silly, and anyway, the use of different colored inks marks you as a nerd. All of that may be true. But if not being a nerd hasn't worked for you, let us suggest you try the opposite.

Seriously, though—marking your outline in this way is the most visual, concrete, and satisfying way of charting your progress toward mastery of all the subject areas in a multiple-choice test. If you don't believe us, *see infra* (as they say in the law).

As we have stressed throughout this book, one of our key goals is to help you to understand and correct your mistakes on multiple-choice exams as efficiently as possible. As you work through the errors and gaps in your substantive knowledge and revise your outlines, we suggest using the following system to ensure you are able to tell when you have mastered the material in your outline and when you are still struggling with a particular subject.[72]

---

72. The suggestions for marking your outline in this section apply to issue, rule, and application gaps in your substantive knowledge.

Steps in Revising the Outline

When you finish a practice exam, for each answer you got wrong because of a substantive knowledge error,

1. identify why you selected the wrong answer (issue? rule? application?);

2. revise the appropriate section of the subject outline to correct the substantive knowledge gap; then

3. make a notation in the margins on that section of your outline by writing both (a) the date you took the practice exam and (b) the question number on your outline *in a different color ink* or in a way that makes the additions to your outline stand out (we use boldface in our example below); *and*

4. keep a record of which practice exams you took on which day so that you can compare answers that you missed on the same topic to look for patterns.

Making notations in the margins helps you test whether you have mastered the revised material when you take your next practice tests.

For example, let's say you are studying for the July administration of the California bar exam.[73] You take a practice exam on 5/31 and miss question 7 on hearsay. First, diagnose why you are missing the question and correct the outline. Then, in the left margin of your hearsay outline, write **5/31, #7**. You take another practice exam on 6/10 and miss question 45 on hearsay. You diagnose why you are missing the question, revise your hearsay outline further if you need to, and on your hearsay outline, write **6/10, #45**. You take another practice exam on 6/22 and miss question 99 on hearsay. Once again, follow the steps and on your hearsay outline, write **6/22, #99**.

---

73. The California bar exam is currently administered over three days during the last week of February and July. Starting in July 2017, it will be administered for two days at the end of July and February.

When you review your outline:

- The dates (5/31, 6/10, and 6/22), tell you whether you have (or have not) mastered the material.

    ○ If you are reviewing your outline on 6/30, the three dates (5/31, 6/10, and 6/22) show you haven't *yet* mastered hearsay. Either you still have a problem with your outline because it is incomplete or incorrect, or you simply haven't yet memorized the new material you added.

    ○ On the other hand, if you are reviewing your outline on 7/20 and have not missed a hearsay question since 6/22, you've probably mastered the hearsay rule.

- The question numbers (7, 45, 99) help you master the material by *pin-pointing your weaknesses*. If you keep missing questions on hearsay, the question numbers allow you to put the missed questions (7, 45, and 99) side-by-side and compare what the fact patterns and pattern of analysis looks like on a hearsay question. By looking at questions that test the same issue, you can learn to recognize fact patterns and patterns of analysis easily.

Over time, these notations will allow you to distinguish between the areas of law you have mastered and the ones you need to continue to work on. This will prevent you from wasting your time continually reviewing areas of law you have already mastered.

The following is an example of what this might look like on an outline after several practice exams on torts.

Issue: Intentional infliction of emotional distress

   Prima facie case:

1. Extreme and outrageous conduct by defendant, *and*
      Rule: The defendant's conduct must be so extreme and outrageous as to be beyond the bounds of decency.
         Consider the following factors:
   a. Abuse of a position of power or authority over plaintiff
   b. (5/31, #21)   Knowledge of plaintiff's susceptibility to distress

    c. Intensity and duration of defendant's conduct

    d. Legitimacy of the defendant's motive

        Note: These are factors—<u>none</u> are required, but all should be considered and must be balanced together.

Is extreme and outrageous:	Is not extreme and outrageous:
<u>Extreme and outrageous conduct</u>: When Sam tells his friend Jim as a joke his wife died in an accident when Jim's wife was actually fine **Note:** Two factors here: intensity of conduct and illegitimate motive **(5/6, #9)** [**Student:** Add other examples with factors here.]	<u>Not extreme and outrageous conduct</u>: When . . . [**Student:** Add examples here.]

2. Intent to cause plaintiff's distress, *and*

    Rule: Defendant must (a) intend to cause the plaintiff severe emotional distress, *or* (b) act with reckless disregard for causing the plaintiff severe emotional distress.

Is reckless:	Is not reckless:
<u>Reckless disregard</u>: When Sam tells his friend Jim his wife died in an accident when Sam knows Jim's wife was actually fine. Is reckless even though Sam didn't intend to cause Jim's heart attack and only wanted to teach Jim a lesson.	<u>No reckless disregard</u>: When . . . [**Student:** Add examples here.]

3. Plaintiff suffered severe emotional distress.
>   **Rule:** Plaintiff must in fact suffer severe emotional distress.
>   Consider the following factors:
>
>   **a.** Intensity and duration of P's distress
>   **b.** (6/7, #37)   Physical manifestations from emotional distress

The notations for **5/31, #21**, and **6/7, #37**, indicate where your outline contained a *rule error* because you missed factors to consider in your rule statements. The notation **5/6, #9**, indicates where you missed choosing the correct answer because of an *application error*.

Using this form of outline notations will help you to focus on the substantive areas that need work. Areas without notations will show you all the areas that you have mastered, allowing you to spend less time on these areas.

CHAPTER 22

How to Use Commercial Materials Effectively

All of the strategies we have given you in this book to improve your multiple-choice exam scores require you to use sample multiple-choice questions to diagnose your weaknesses. Where do you get these questions?

Besides old exam questions from your professors, the main sources of sample multiple-choice questions are from commercial outlines or course supplements and bar preparation materials. Usually these materials are well drafted and are relevant to your specific courses—but not always.[74] Commercial materials may not be updated as quickly as the information you learned in class. To save money, students sometimes rely on older versions of commercial materials passed on by other students that contain some outdated law. When questions in commercial materials are poorly drafted, they can confuse you and slow down your learning process by making you review law you already know. Questions in commercial materials may also be irrelevant to you because they include topics not covered by your professor. You need to know how to identify these questions so you can ignore them and move on. In this final chapter, we give you strategies to avoid some of the pitfalls posed by these commercial materials both for law school exams and for the bar exam.

---

74. This is why the MBE always includes questions that aren't counted in your score; the drafters are testing whether they are clearly drafted.

PREPARING FOR A LAW SCHOOL EXAM

When you are using practice questions from commercial materials to study for a law school exam and you miss a question, ask yourself the following questions.

- Was this material covered by the professor in class or assigned in the class reading?

- Are the rules for the question and its answers subject to interpretation?

- Is the question poorly written?

Was the material covered by the professor?

You must first ask yourself "Was this material covered by the professor in class or assigned in the class reading?" because not all topics covered by the MBE or commercial study aids are covered by professors in their law school courses. The scope of commercial multiple-choice questions may be broader than your professor's course coverage. For instance, if the torts question you missed is a privacy torts question about intrusion upon seclusion, but your class only covered public disclosure of private facts, then that question is irrelevant for your class exam and you should ignore it.

Is the material subject to interpretation?

Next, if the subject *is* one you covered in class, then ask, "Are the rules for the question and its answers subject to interpretation?" Many legal rules and their elements are broken down differently by different professors when they teach them in their classes. This can cause confusion if the way the commercial materials' author broke down a rule varies from your professor's way.

For example, some professors or authors may break negligence into the following four elements.

Negligence—four elements:

1. Duty: Does the defendant owe plaintiff a duty?

2. Breach: If a duty is owed, *what is the standard of care*, and did defendant breach it?

3. Causation: Was defendant's breach of duty the actual and proximate cause of harm to plaintiff?

4. Damages: Did the plaintiff suffer damages?

Other professors, however, may break negligence into basically the same elements and interpret the elements differently:

Negligence—five elements with a different interpretation:

1. Duty: Does the defendant owe plaintiff a duty, and if so, *what is the standard of care*?

2. Breach: Did defendant's conduct fall below the standard of care?

3. Actual causation: Did defendant's conduct actually cause harm to plaintiff?

4. Proximate causation: Did defendant's conduct proximately cause harm to plaintiff?

5. Damages: Did the plaintiff suffer damages?

If your professor uses the first rule formulation (where the concept of standard of care is included in the breach element) but the commercial question you missed uses the second formulation, the following answer choice may confuse you.

a. Defendant owed no duty to provide aid to plaintiff by calling 911.

You may have missed the question because the correct answer choice relied on the second formulation, which includes the standard of care under the first element—duty. You were using the first formulation you learned in class that includes standard of care in the breach element. Thus, the above answer choice is *subject to interpretation* depending on which rule formula you are using.

How can you identify where an issue is subject to interpretation? It will appear in the *explanation* for the correct answer supplied by the authors of the commercial material. In that explanation you would see the second formulation of the rule. In such a case, you would then review your notes to be sure you are interpreting the answer the way *your professor* would—using the first formulation where the standard of care is considered under the breach element.

Is the question poorly written?

If the material was covered in class and the answers are not subject to interpretation but you still missed the question, the last thing to ask yourself is whether the question was poorly written. It is hard to draft a good multiple-choice question that has one clear answer choice but is not so easy that a student can answer it correctly with minimal knowledge. While trying to test nuances in the law, a professor may inadvertently create a fact pattern that raises unintentional legal issues or ambiguities. As a result, many multiple-choice questions can be poorly drafted and confusing.

How can you tell when a question is poorly drafted? Take a look at the answer choices and at the author's explanation for the correct answer. If you know and understand the law but you can't logically follow how the author arrived at the answer using the facts in the problem, there may be a drafting problem. Look at the facts in the problem and in the answer and ask the following questions.

- Are the facts (in the fact pattern or in the answers choices) ambiguous?

- Are there enough facts in the problem to support the correct answer?

- Does the explanation seem to rely on facts that aren't clear in the fact pattern or in the answers?

If you answered "yes" to any of these questions, chances are that this question may be poorly drafted.[75] If the question is badly written, you can simple discard the question and move on. Be careful here, though: If you notice that you identify many similar questions as poorly written, you want to go back and check to make sure that is true. It is more likely that you have a reading problem or a substantive knowledge problem.

If you answered "no" to these three questions, then you likely missed the correct answer because of a reading problem (Chapter 13) or a substantive knowledge problem (Chapter 17). In that case, start at Chapter 12, "What Am I Doing Wrong?" Use that chapter to help you diagnose your specific weaknesses.

PREPARING FOR THE MULTISTATE BAR EXAM

To decide which commercial multiple-choice questions you may ignore when you are studying for the bar exam, you should take a slightly different approach than you would when you are studying for a law school exam. As a law student, you have to tailor your performance for each professor when you are taking that professor's exam. In contrast, when you are studying for the bar exam, you must tailor your knowledge and your answers to the guidelines outlined by the National Conference of Bar Examiners who oversee the creation of the exam. This means your questions become these.

- Is this material within the bar exam's scope of coverage?

- Is the question subject to interpretation?

---

75. If you have any doubts, check with your professor and/or with your study group to be sure.

Is this material within the bar exam's scope of coverage?

Before taking practice tests to prepare for the bar exam, be sure to familiarize yourself with the scope of coverage of all subjects as set forth by the Committee of Bar Examiners *for the test you are about to take.* The scope of coverage of the bar exam does change, so you need to be particularly careful about changes in the scope of coverage when you are using older/outdated bar exam study guides. Also, multiple-choice questions in the Examples and Explanations series (Aspen) and in commercial outlines or study aids created primarily to help you with classroom performance may offer practice multiple-choice questions on topics that are *not covered* by the MBE.[76] Check the National Committee of Bar Examiners Web site for up-to-date information (http://www.ncbex.org).

Is the question subject to interpretation?

If the material in the practice question you missed is within the MBE's scope of coverage, you want to ask yourself whether the question is subject to interpretation. As explained above, you want to determine whether you chose a wrong answer because you interpreted the answers based on the way your professor broke down the rule when the bar examiners are using a different breakdown of the rule. If the answer is yes, then you need to *write this difference on your outline and memorize it.* Note that this is different than what you should do when you are preparing for a law school exam where you want to follow your professor's model. This time, you need to change your breakdown and application of the rule in your outline so that it matches the bar examiners' reasoning in the explanations given for the correct answer; bar examiners will expect you to apply the same interpretation that they do.

Similarly, when preparing for the MBE, if the material in the practice question falls within the scope of the bar exam and the answers are not subject to interpretation but you still missed the question, you cannot

---

76. These questions may still be relevant for individual state bar exams or for legal practice.

simply ignore the missed question because you think it is poorly written. Although some multiple-choice questions on the bar exam are not counted because they are being tested for the first time, you the test taker will never know which questions they are. Consequently, you still need to study questions that you believe are poorly written to review how the bar examiners are interpreting the facts and why they believe a particular answer is correct. In other words, when studying for the MBE, *assume the error is a lack of substantive knowledge and correct your outline accordingly,* even if you think the question is poorly written.

A WORD OF CAUTION

In addition to using commercial materials for the sample multiple-choice questions they contain, many students also use commercial outlines to create their own study outlines for their classes. We always tell students to be careful when using commercial materials to write their outlines; commercial outlines are most useful as a way to check that your own outline is correct. Creating your outline from scratch is one of the most helpful ways to learn the rules and synthesize your understanding of the law. Don't simply copy the rules from a commercial outline. First try to formulate them yourself using your class notes and your casebook, and then compare your rules to the statements of the law in the commercial materials. Remember that some commercial outlines are better than others, both in terms of accuracy and thoroughness, so you should never simply copy material from the commercial outline without critically examining its contents.

A FINAL NOTE ON COMMERCIAL MATERIALS

Commercial materials are useful as a resource for information whether studying for a law school exam or for the bar exam. However, these materials should be not be used without understanding their strengths and limitations. Use commercial material critically, keeping in mind the reason why you are using them—for a law school exam or for the bar exam.

CHAPTER 23

A Final Note on Using the System

I stop somewhere, waiting for you.
— Walt Whitman

One conviction underlies our work as academic support professionals: If a student wants to be an attorney and has put the work in to attend, survive, and graduate law school—that student deserves to be a lawyer. So, to the extent that this book helps or has helped you in that ambition, let us say (possibly well in advance): Welcome to a really great profession. Being an attorney is one of the best things in the world.

This book has outlined a systematic approach to improving your multiple-choice performance. While it can seem time consuming and, at times, tedious, we believe that in the long run it is the quickest way to pinpoint and correct your weaknesses. It will also help you to make the most efficient use of your limited study time to prepare for your multiple-choice exams. As an added bonus, many of the strategies in this book will also improve your performance on your law school essay exams, since better time management and better reading and substantive knowledge skills will make you better prepared to issue-spot and analyze essay questions.

Applying the skills in this book will help you to earn better grades in law school and to pass the Multistate Bar Exam and the Multistate Professional Responsibility Exam. But we believe the benefits you will obtain by mastering these skills can go beyond merely improving your law school performance because these are skills lawyers continue to use throughout their careers. For example, the outlining strategies from Chapter 21 can help you to understand and organize legal issues you encounter in practice. The IRAC strategies discussed in Part Three can strengthen your legal analysis in your legal writing and oral arguments. And the time management strategies from Part One can be adapted to help manage the many demands on your time when you enter law practice. Taking the time to master the skills discussed in this book will be worth the effort.

From time management to the final notations to pinpoint and correct your errors, this system was created through years of trial and error with the help of many, many, many law students and bar exam students. We couldn't have created this system without them working with us to design it. So to all of them—thank you for your trust in us.

To all of you reading this book, we believe this system will work for you too. If you have read through the book before trying the system, there's no need to say *caveat emptor*.[77] At this point, it's more like *festina lente*—time to get started.[78] There's no substitute for working through the system, and you won't know whether it works until you do that.

If this book has helped you, then do *us* a favor: Introduce or, better still, explain it to a friend who is also struggling with multiple-choice exams. Although there are side benefits to learning a multiple-choice system, the first goal is the most important one: pass the exam, get your degree, pass the bar, become an attorney. The people who are willing to put in the work to learn this system and to endure the tests that the bar exam imposes on them—those are the people who should be attorneys. So help out your friends and future colleagues, and help make more good lawyers. We, and all of our colleagues, will be here to welcome you into the profession.

---

77. "Let the buyer beware."
78. "Hurry slowly."

Exam First Aid—Self-Diagnostic Questionnaire

EXAM FIRST AID—SELF-DIAGNOSTIC QUESTIONNAIRE

Time Management	The Approach	Evaluating Performance and Diagnosing Problems
Before the Exam 1. Did you finish your substantive outlines? 2. Did you have enough time to "test your outlines" for accuracy on a practice exam? 3. Did you have enough time to memorize your outline? 4. Did you have enough time to "test your knowledge" on a practice exam? During the Exam 1. Did you finish the exam? 2. Did you have enough time to correctly mark your Scantron? 3. Did you have enough time to review only the questions where you were unsure of the answer?	Do you have an approach strategy for questions that allows you to 1. narrow the issue(s) before reading the fact pattern; 2. separate the possible answers from the improbable ones; and 3. among questions, distinguish between certain vs. uncertain answers?	Do you have a system[79] for evaluating your incorrect answer to determine whether the answer is incorrect because of 1. reading problems; 2. a lack of substantive knowledge; and/or 3. confusion from using commercial materials?
If yes, no problem. But if no, then see **Part One**.	If yes, no problem. But if no, then see **Part Two**.	If yes, no problem. But if no, then see **Part Three**.

---

79. Simply reading the correct answer and mentally noting why you missed the question is not a sufficient system to enable you to improve your multiple-choice scores. Making a mental notation and doing nothing more indicates a belief that you will forever remember the mistake you made and will not repeat it.

PART ONE—TIME MANAGEMENT

Before the exam

For a doctrinal class, studying involves the following:

- Step 1—*Before class*: read and brief the cases.

- Step 2—Attend and participate in lecture.

- Step 3—*After class*: correct your briefs, fill in holes in your lecture notes ("note-holes"), and attend your professor's office hours to clear-up any confusion.

- Step 4—Outline the course materials.

- Step 5—Test your outline on a practice exam *before* you memorize it.

- Step 6—Assess your outline—did it work for you?

- Step 7—*About a month before exams*: memorize your outline, condense your outline into a checklist, and look for issues that relate to each other.

- Step 8—Test your knowledge (your memorization) on a practice exam.

If you did not have enough time to finish your substantive outlines (Step 4), test the outlines for accuracy on a practice exam (Steps 5 and 6), memorize your outlines (Step 7), *or* test your knowledge on a practice exam (Step 8), then you are not allocating enough time to "study."[80]

To allocate more hours to studying:

1. Figure out how you are spending your time every day. Keep track of your activities for 24/7—24 hours, for 7 days.

2. Determine what activities are negotiable versus nonnegotiable. For example, classroom and commute time are usually

---

80. Remember, the rule of thumb is that for every hour in class, you spend three to four hours outside of class studying.

nonnegotiable. But spending two hours exercising every day is negotiable. Can you instead exercise one hour every day or two hours every two days?

Note about sleep: You know how much sleep you need to feel refreshed and mentally sharp. Cutting down on sleep is not a good idea. It makes you cranky and, more important, mentally less sharp, making it harder for you to learn and retain information. While some sleep deprivation may be necessary during the day or two before exams, it should not be a regular practice.

3. Determine how many hours during the week you can actually spend studying. Then ask—

"Am I comfortable with my level of commitment to my *goal* of becoming a lawyer?"

If no, then use what you learned about how you spend your time to free up more time to study by modifying the times that are negotiable.

4. Using a monthly calendar, map out your semester. Include the following:

   - All academic dates and deadlines set by your professors or your school—midterms, legal writing papers, finals, etc.

   - All self-imposed deadlines such as completing your outline (Step 4), taking a practice exam to test your outline (Step 5), etc.

   - Extracurricular academic workshops—Academic Support outlining workshop, professor's substantive review session, etc.

   - School holidays and breaks

5. Daily calendar and monthly calendar work together. The daily calendar tells you *when* you have time to study. The monthly calendar tells you *what* you should be doing during that study time.

Note about multitasking and overlapping steps

Outlining: You should start your outline after your professor has finished lecturing on an informational unit, such as "offer" in contracts. Once the professor has finished lecturing on that topic, you have about 95 percent of all you need to know about "offer." The other 5 percent comes from how offer interacts with other issues, such as acceptance or the defense of mutual mistake.

Multitasking: This means what while you are doing Steps 1 through 3 on another informational unit, such as acceptance, you will be working an offer through Step 4, then 5, and finally 6. And the same is true in every doctrinal class you take.

During the exam—create your exam strategy

Before beginning to answer the exam, *scan the entire exam* to determine how to allocate your time based on

- the types of questions;

- the number of questions;

- if indicated, the time allotted for each question; and

- if indicated, the weighted value for each question.

With the multiple-choice portion of the exam

1. Mark your time allocation for the exam at reasonable intervals. Use the time allocations to pace your work.

Example 1

Assume you have to answer 100 multiple-choice questions in two hours. Your exam starts at noon and ends at 2:00 p.m. Before beginning to answer the questions, mark your exam book as follows:

- at question 25, write **12:30 p.m.**

- at question 50, write **1:00 p.m.**

- at question 75, write **1:30 p.m.**

- at question 100, write **2:00 p.m.**

Note: This time strategy assumes you are marking your Scantron as you answer each question. No time has been allocated for marking the Scantron at the end. In addition, no time has been allocated to review questions where you are unsure of your answer choice. If you want time to either mark your Scantron at the end or to review questions where you are unsure of your answer, *change your exam strategy* to account for the time.

Example 2

Assume the facts of the exam are the same as above. But you usually experience some mild test anxiety and it takes you a few minutes to get composed and focused on the exam. *Change your exam strategy* to include the time you need. For example, if you gave yourself five minutes, your timing would look like this:

- at question 25, write **12:34 p.m.**

- at question 50, write **1:03 p.m.**

- at question 75, write **1:31 p.m.**

- at question 100, write **2:00 p.m.**

   Changing your exam strategy to build in what you need to stay focused on the exam is powerful. It takes into consideration how you work and puts you in control of the exam situation.

2. ALWAYS stick to your time allocations.

   In Example 1 above, when you come to question 25 in the exam, check your time. If you are at 12:30, you are on track. If you are at 12:35, you need to pick up speed. If you are at 12:20, you can slow down.

PART TWO—THE APPROACH

Step 1—Scan the call of the question and the answers

Before you read the fact pattern, *quickly scan the call of the question and the answer choices* to look for legal terms that give you clues to the issues or causes of action that will be raised in the fact pattern. In *law school*, a quick scan will enable you to determine the issues being tested before reading the fact pattern. On the *bar exam*, a quick scan will enable you to determine the area of law *and* the issues being tested before reading the fact pattern.

Example 1

If Smith *killed* Hardy because of the threat to his own life, Smith should be found

a. not guilty, because of the *defense of duress.*

b. not guilty, because of the *defense of necessity.*

c. guilty of *first-degree murder.*

d. guilty of *second-degree murder.*

By quickly scanning the call of the question and the answer choices first, you can read the fact pattern knowing that the topic of the question is criminal law—homicide and defenses of duress and necessity. The issues presented are those italicized above for emphasis. Those words are the words you are scanning for in the call of the question and the answer choices.

Example 2

Wallingford's testimony is

a. admissible as a *present sense impression.*

b. admissible to *impeach* Minter.

c. inadmissible, because Perez may not *impeach* his own witness.

d. inadmissible, because it is *hearsay* not with any exception.

By quickly scanning the answer choices first, you can read the fact pattern knowing that the topic of the question is evidence—impeachment, hearsay, and hearsay exceptions. The issues are italicized above for emphasis.

Step 2—Read the fact pattern and mark legal issues, facts, and categories

After scanning the call of the question and the answer choices, *read the fact pattern* and mark it up as you would an essay question. Actively read for the facts relating to the issues raised in the call of the question and the answer choices.

Read each sentence in the fact pattern systematically, critically, and aggressively.

- Ask yourself: Why is this sentence in the fact pattern?

- Look for facts that relate to the issues mentioned in the call of the question and the answer choices. Circle or underline the facts and identify the issue.

- If you are unclear about the issues from the answer choices, read the fact pattern and ask whether any fact(s) in the sentence trigger those issues. Be sure to circle or underline the facts and identify the issue you believe the facts trigger.

Step 3—Read the call of the question and the answer choices

Read the call of the question and ALL the answer choices carefully. Circle key words that indicate conditions (e.g. if, only if, unless, not, must, may, etc.) OR words that narrows choices (because, best answer, worst answer, most likely, least likely, etc.)

Step 4—Answer the question

Eliminate obvious wrong answers. (*Hint:* One way to eliminate wrong answers is to mark each answer as "true" or "false." Eliminate all false answers.)

If you have more than one possible answer, make an educated guess *and* mark the question number by circling the number. The circled question number indicates you are unsure of your answer.

Step 5—Finish the test, then review

If you have time to review your answers, *only* go back and review the answers to the circled question numbers. Do not go back and review all your answers to all the questions. Reviewing all the questions will lead to changing the right answer to the wrong one because you did not have enough time to consider the question thoroughly the second time around.

When reviewing the circled question numbers:

- Reread the *entire* question as if you are reading it for the first time— scan the call of the question and the answer choices, read and mark the fact pattern, read the call of the question and the answer choices, eliminate the wrong answers, and then make an educated guess. (*Hint:* Use another color pen or pencil to help you distinguish the second read from your first read.)

- If your second answer choice is the same your first answer choice, stick with your answer.

- If your second answer choice is different from your first, mark the question number again, change your answer, *and* if time permits, repeat the process a third time.

PART THREE—EVALUATING PERFORMANCE AND DIAGNOSING PROBLEMS

Reading problem

Determine where your reading is off.

- Did you misread the call of the question?

- Did you misread the answer choices?

- Did you misread the fact pattern?

If yes to any of the above:

- Check your time allocations and be sure you are giving yourself enough time to carefully read the question.

- Practice reading calls of the question to determine what is being asked for you to decide.

- Circle or underline key words that you are misreading in the answer choices and/or fact patterns. Look for trends/similarities in the questions you misread. These may include words that indicate conditions (e.g., *if, only if, and, or*) or words that narrow choices (e.g., *unless, not, must, may, because*).

Notes

1. If you can answer the questions correctly with *additional time*, and this is true in all your classes, consider being tested for a learning disability.

2. If you can answer the questions correctly once you are relaxed and out of the test environment, consider speaking to a professional (psychologist or doctor) about test anxiety.

Lack of substantive knowledge

IRAC, IRAC, IRAC: When you miss an answer, determine why. Use IRAC because selecting an incorrect answer means you reached the wrong conclusion.

Ask yourself:

- Did I miss the *Issue* in the fact pattern?

- Did I miss the *Rule*?

- Did I miss the *Application* of the rule to the fact pattern?

Notes

1. Always analyze your incorrect answer by looking first for the I, then the R, and then the A. Once you identify the problem, stop. For example, if you cannot identify the correct issue, you cannot select the correct answer. If you spotted the issue but don't know the rule, then you are unlikely to choose the correct answer.

2. *Warning:* Do not assume the problem is always with the R. It is not uncommon for students to be able to recite the rule but to be unable to identify the I or to make mistakes in the A.

Revising your outline

Once you determine why you selected the wrong answer, make a notation on your outline by writing (a) the date you took the practice exam, and (b) the question number on your outline *in a different color ink* or in way that makes the additions to your outline stand out.

Example:

You are studying for the bar exam. You take a practice exam on 5/31 and miss question 7 on hearsay. On your hearsay outline, identify why you missed the question, revise your outline, and write **5/31, #7.** You take another practice exam on 6/10 and miss question 45 on hearsay. Revise your hearsay outline and write **6/10, #45.** You take another practice exam on 6/22 and miss question 99 on hearsay. Revise your hearsay outline and write **6/22, #99.**

On reviewing your outline:

- The dates (5/31, 6/10, and 6/22) tell you whether you have mastered the material. If you are reviewing your outline on 6/30, the three dates show you haven't *yet* mastered hearsay. However, if you are reviewing your outline on 7/20 and have not missed a hearsay question since 6/22, you have probably mastered the hearsay rule.

- The question numbers (7, 45, 99) help you master the material. If you keep missing questions on hearsay, the question numbers allow you to put the missed questions (7, 45, and 99) side by side and compare what the fact pattern and pattern of analysis look like on a hearsay question. By looking at questions that test the same issue, you can learn to recognize fact patterns and patterns of analysis.

Over time, notating your outline will allow you to distinguish between the areas of law you have mastered and the ones you need to continue working on. Don't waste your time continually reviewing areas of law you have already mastered.

If you missed the issue:

Add the key facts that trigger the issue to your outline by inserting a box just above the rule. Inside the box, write **Issue looks like**. Then write the date, question number, and the key facts that triggered the issue.

You also may need to add the key facts to the issue you incorrectly believed was triggered by inserting a box just above the rule. Inside the box, write **Issue does not look like**. Then again, write the date, question number, and the key facts that you incorrectly believed triggered the issue.

Example:

David shouted, "Tomorrow, I'm coming back and I'm going to beat you until you're black and blue."

- If you identified this as raising the issue of assault, then write the fact pattern in the assault section of your outline as an example of what assault does *not* factually look like.

- If you did not identify this as raising the issue of an intentional infliction of emotional distress (IIED), then write the fact pattern in the IIED section of your outline as an example of what IIED factually looks like.

If you missed the rule:

Check to see whether the rule on your outline is correct, complete (includes exceptions, factors, etc.), and concisely written.

- If incorrect, correct the rule. Again, be sure to write the date and the question number. If you are using old practice exams, the law may have changed. In *law school*, if in doubt about the correct formulation of the rule, check with the professor. For the *bar exam*, refer to the study outline.

- If correct, you haven't memorized the rule. Highlight the rule, write it on a flashcard, and work on your memorization.

Note: If you don't have enough time to memorize the rule accurately, this is a time management problem before the exam.

If you missed the analysis:

After the rule, add the key facts *and* the analysis (reasoning) to your outline so that you have a pattern of analysis to study in the future.

If the problem is one of value judgments (e.g., most likely, least likely, best argument, least helpful argument), then make a note of how the correct answer is selected. Remember, the law is based on value judgments and often prioritizes them.

Example 1

General value judgments

- Procedure before substance.

- Legal before equitable.

- Defeating the prima facie case is better than a successful defense, even though they both result in the defendant prevailing in the lawsuit.

Example 2

Subject-based value judgments

- Torts: For the plaintiff, an intentional tort claim is better than one for negligence because of the availability of punitive damages.

- Constitutional law: For the plaintiff, a substantive due process claim may be better than one for equal protection because a substantive due process claim means that government must stop its action vs. only acting in a way that does not discriminate.

Example 3

Policy-based value judgments

- Contracts: Ambiguous contract terms are construed against the drafter.

- Property: Law prefers the free alienability of property.

Confusion from using commercial materials:

For a *law school exam*, when using commercial multiple-choice questions and you missed a question, consider:

1. Was the material covered in class? If no, no problem. The scope of a commercial multiple-choice question may be broader than the course coverage.
   If yes, then . . .

2. Is the question subject to interpretation? If yes, review your lecture notes and determine how your professor would interpret the answer choices.
   If no, then . . .

3. Is the question poorly written? If no, check for substantive or reading error.
   If yes, articulate why you believe the answer was poorly written.

For a *bar exam*, when using commercial multiple-choice questions and you missed a question:

1. Assume the material is within the scope of coverage on the bar exam *unless* the Committee of Bar Examiners indicates otherwise.

2. If the question is subject to interpretation, review how the examiners are interpreting the facts and why a particular answer choice is correct.

3. If the question is poorly written, review how the bar examiners are interpreting the facts and why a particular answer choice is correct.

In other words, for purpose of the bar exam, *assume* the error is due to 2a lack of substantive knowledge and correct accordingly.

Time Management Charts

How Do I Spend My Time?
(Daily Calendar)

Plan on spending for each hour in class *at least* three to four hours per week outside of class studying. This means that 15 units = 45 hours per week studying, and 9 units = 27 hours per week studying.

Studying is defined as

1. class preparation,

2. legal research and working on your legal writing paper,

3. working on course outlines,

4. taking practice exams,

5. working in study groups, and

6. meeting with your professors to discuss the material.

Studying is *not*

1. "hanging out" on campus;

2. meeting with student groups (e.g., Student Bar Association, Environmental Law Society, Law Students for Serious Partying), or

3. socializing in the library, in the quad, after class, or anywhere else.

To plan your studies realistically, with the daily calendar:

First:

For *each* day, mark the time you spend

1. in class,

2. taking care of *physical* needs (e.g., eating, sleeping, exercising, hygiene),

3. taking care of *spiritual* needs (e.g., church, meditation),

4. taking care of *emotional* needs (e.g., family, friends),

5. taking care of *mental* needs (school not included) (e.g., recreational reading), and

6. taking care of *financial* needs (e.g., work!).

Second:

Plan out your study times and then add up the number of hours. Are you comfortable with your level of commitment to your goal of becoming a lawyer? If not, now is the time to prioritize.

Be honest and realistic!

MONDAY

6:00 AM		6:30 PM	
6:30 AM		7:00 PM	
7:00 AM		7:30 PM	
7:30 AM		8:00 PM	
8:00 AM		8:30 PM	
8:30 AM		9:00 PM	
9:00 AM		9:30 PM	
9:30 AM		10:00 PM	
10:00 AM		10:30 PM	
10:30 AM		11:00 PM	
11:00 AM		11:30 PM	
11:30 AM		12:00 AM	
12:00 PM		12:30 AM	
12:30 PM		1:00 AM	
1:00 PM		1:30 AM	
1:30 PM		2:00 AM	
2:00 PM		2:30 AM	
2:30 PM		3:00 AM	
3:00 PM		3:30 AM	
3:30 PM		4:00 AM	
4:00 PM		4:30 AM	
4:30 PM		5:00 AM	
5:00 PM		5:30 AM	
5:30 PM		6:00 AM	
6:00 PM			

TUESDAY

6:00 AM		6:30 PM	
6:30 AM		7:00 PM	
7:00 AM		7:30 PM	
7:30 AM		8:00 PM	
8:00 AM		8:30 PM	
8:30 AM		9:00 PM	
9:00 AM		9:30 PM	
9:30 AM		10:00 PM	
10:00 AM		10:30 PM	
10:30 AM		11:00 PM	
11:00 AM		11:30 PM	
11:30 AM		12:00 AM	
12:00 PM		12:30 AM	
12:30 PM		1:00 AM	
1:00 PM		1:30 AM	
1:30 PM		2:00 AM	
2:00 PM		2:30 AM	
2:30 PM		3:00 AM	
3:00 PM		3:30 AM	
3:30 PM		4:00 AM	
4:00 PM		4:30 AM	
4:30 PM		5:00 AM	
5:00 PM		5:30 AM	
5:30 PM		6:00 AM	
6:00 PM			

Wednesday

6:00 AM		6:30 PM	
6:30 AM		7:00 PM	
7:00 AM		7:30 PM	
7:30 AM		8:00 PM	
8:00 AM		8:30 PM	
8:30 AM		9:00 PM	
9:00 AM		9:30 PM	
9:30 AM		10:00 PM	
10:00 AM		10:30 PM	
10:30 AM		11:00 PM	
11:00 AM		11:30 PM	
11:30 AM		12:00 AM	
12:00 PM		12:30 AM	
12:30 PM		1:00 AM	
1:00 PM		1:30 AM	
1:30 PM		2:00 AM	
2:00 PM		2:30 AM	
2:30 PM		3:00 AM	
3:00 PM		3:30 AM	
3:30 PM		4:00 AM	
4:00 PM		4:30 AM	
4:30 PM		5:00 AM	
5:00 PM		5:30 AM	
5:30 PM		6:00 AM	
6:00 PM			

THURSDAY

6:00 AM		6:30 PM	
6:30 AM		7:00 PM	
7:00 AM		7:30 PM	
7:30 AM		8:00 PM	
8:00 AM		8:30 PM	
8:30 AM		9:00 PM	
9:00 AM		9:30 PM	
9:30 AM		10:00 PM	
10:00 AM		10:30 PM	
10:30 AM		11:00 PM	
11:00 AM		11:30 PM	
11:30 AM		12:00 AM	
12:00 PM		12:30 AM	
12:30 PM		1:00 AM	
1:00 PM		1:30 AM	
1:30 PM		2:00 AM	
2:00 PM		2:30 AM	
2:30 PM		3:00 AM	
3:00 PM		3:30 AM	
3:30 PM		4:00 AM	
4:00 PM		4:30 AM	
4:30 PM		5:00 AM	
5:00 PM		5:30 AM	
5:30 PM		6:00 AM	
6:00 PM			

Friday

6:00 AM		6:30 PM	
6:30 AM		7:00 PM	
7:00 AM		7:30 PM	
7:30 AM		8:00 PM	
8:00 AM		8:30 PM	
8:30 AM		9:00 PM	
9:00 AM		9:30 PM	
9:30 AM		10:00 PM	
10:00 AM		10:30 PM	
10:30 AM		11:00 PM	
11:00 AM		11:30 PM	
11:30 AM		12:00 AM	
12:00 PM		12:30 AM	
12:30 PM		1:00 AM	
1:00 PM		1:30 AM	
1:30 PM		2:00 AM	
2:00 PM		2:30 AM	
2:30 PM		3:00 AM	
3:00 PM		3:30 AM	
3:30 PM		4:00 AM	
4:00 PM		4:30 AM	
4:30 PM		5:00 AM	
5:00 PM		5:30 AM	
5:30 PM		6:00 AM	
6:00 PM			

SATURDAY

6:00 AM		6:30 PM	
6:30 AM		7:00 PM	
7:00 AM		7:30 PM	
7:30 AM		8:00 PM	
8:00 AM		8:30 PM	
8:30 AM		9:00 PM	
9:00 AM		9:30 PM	
9:30 AM		10:00 PM	
10:00 AM		10:30 PM	
10:30 AM		11:00 PM	
11:00 AM		11:30 PM	
11:30 AM		12:00 AM	
12:00 PM		12:30 AM	
12:30 PM		1:00 AM	
1:00 PM		1:30 AM	
1:30 PM		2:00 AM	
2:00 PM		2:30 AM	
2:30 PM		3:00 AM	
3:00 PM		3:30 AM	
3:30 PM		4:00 AM	
4:00 PM		4:30 AM	
4:30 PM		5:00 AM	
5:00 PM		5:30 AM	
5:30 PM		6:00 AM	
6:00 PM			

SUNDAY

6:00 AM		6:30 PM	
6:30 AM		7:00 PM	
7:00 AM		7:30 PM	
7:30 AM		8:00 PM	
8:00 AM		8:30 PM	
8:30 AM		9:00 PM	
9:00 AM		9:30 PM	
9:30 AM		10:00 PM	
10:00 AM		10:30 PM	
10:30 AM		11:00 PM	
11:00 AM		11:30 PM	
11:30 AM		12:00 AM	
12:00 PM		12:30 AM	
12:30 PM		1:00 AM	
1:00 PM		1:30 AM	
1:30 PM		2:00 AM	
2:00 PM		2:30 AM	
2:30 PM		3:00 AM	
3:00 PM		3:30 AM	
3:30 PM		4:00 AM	
4:00 PM		4:30 AM	
4:30 PM		5:00 AM	
5:00 PM		5:30 AM	
5:30 PM		6:00 AM	
6:00 PM			

How Do I Manage My Time?
(Monthly Calendar)

Get an idea of what your academic semester will look like at the *start* of the semester. By knowing what to expect *during* your semester, you can plan ahead.

Complete the attached monthly calendar of your semester by doing the following.

1. Starting backward by calendaring information on your end-of-semester exams for each class. If possible, find out

   - date;

   - time;

   - location;

   - type of exam (essay only, multiple choice only, or a combination); and

   - if applicable, weight of the exam (e.g., 25 percent midterm).

   Knowing information about your exams will help you to naturally prioritize your work. For example, if your first exam is a property 100 percent final exam, you will want to work on your property outline first. However, if the first exam is a property 25 percent midterm but the second exam is a torts 100 percent final exam, you will want to work on your torts outline before your property outline.

2. Calendar dates of any midterm exams.

3. Calendar dates your legal writing papers are due.

4. Calendar dates of any ex-curricular workshops such as Academic Support outlining or exam writing workshops and substantive course review sessions.

5. Calendar school holidays and breaks.

Once you have completed your calendar, you will have, at a glance, an idea of what tasks need to be completed on a *weekly* basis. This calendar, combined with your *daily* calendars (that identify your "study times") should enable you to identify the tasks that need to be completed as well as the order (prioritizing) of completing them.

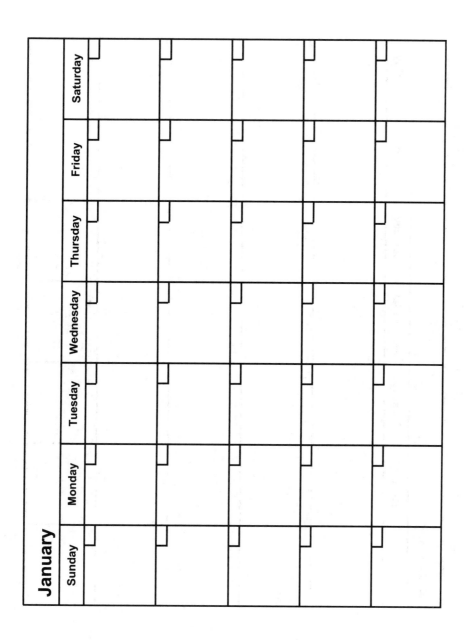

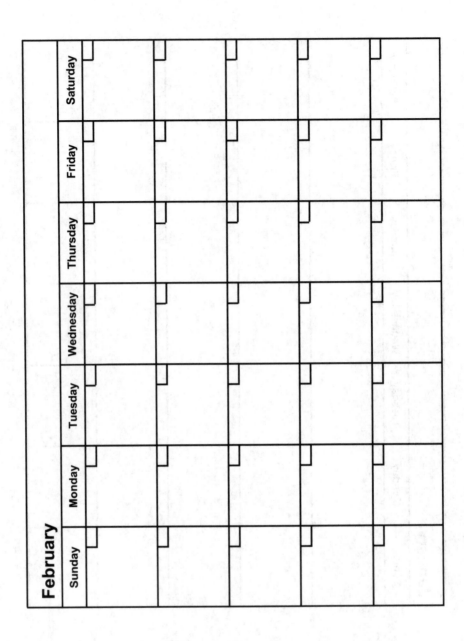

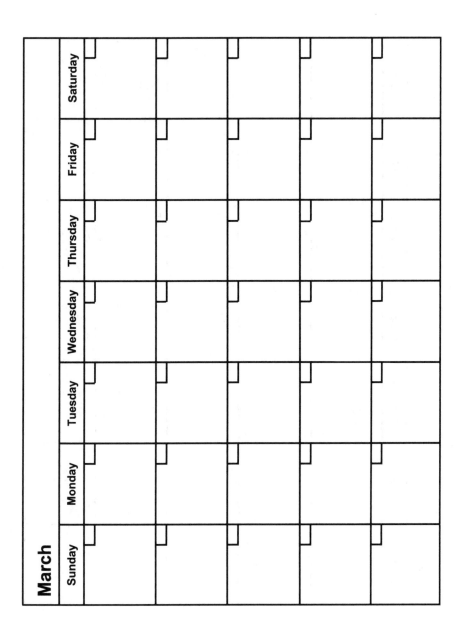

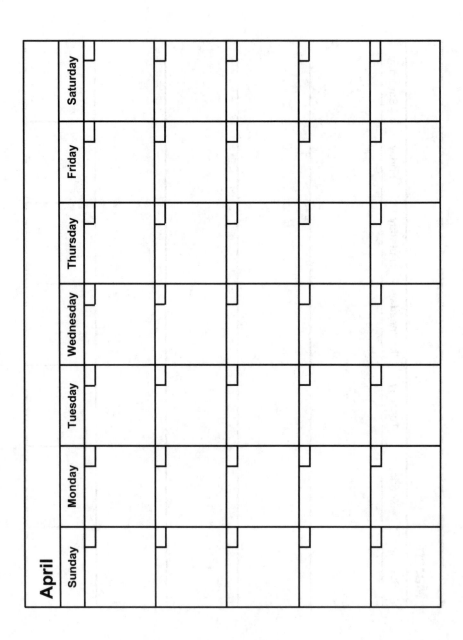

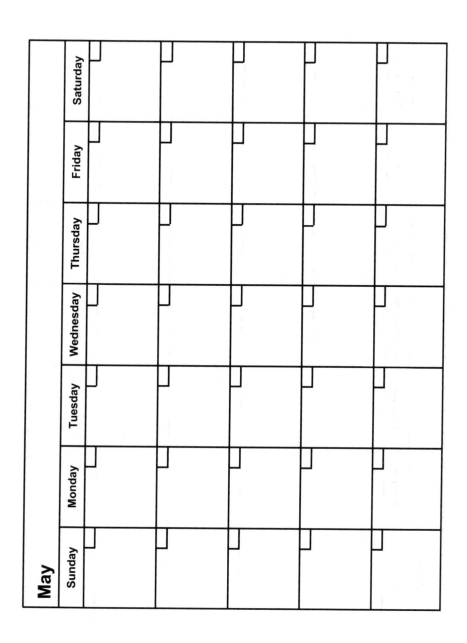

May

Sunday	Monday	Tuesday	Wednesday	Thursday	Friday	Saturday

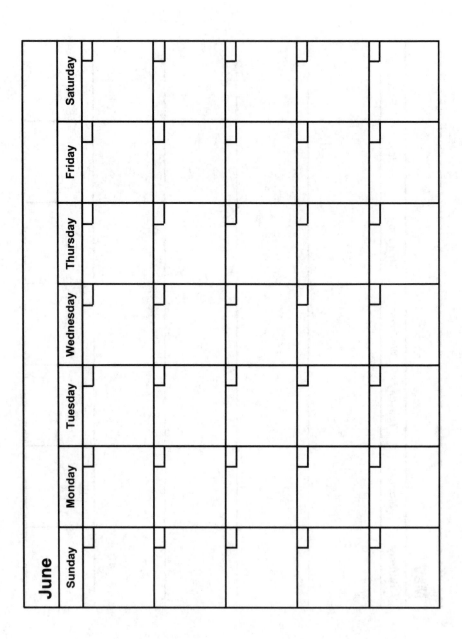

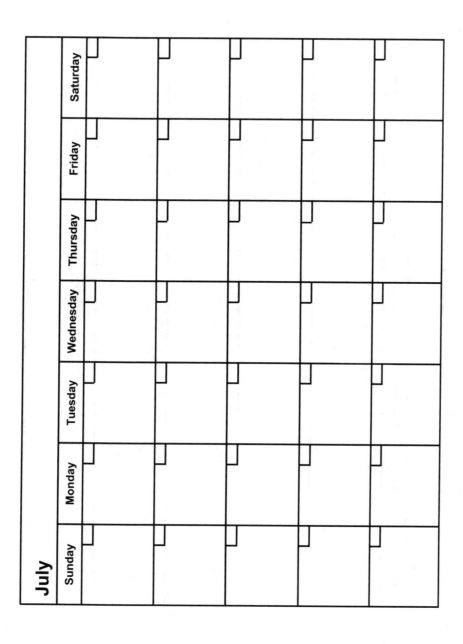

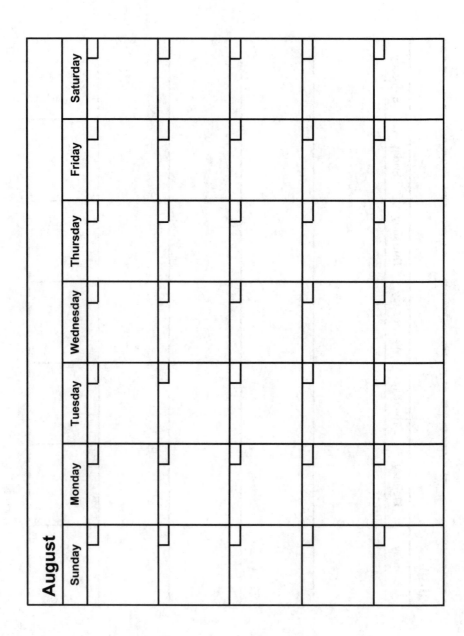

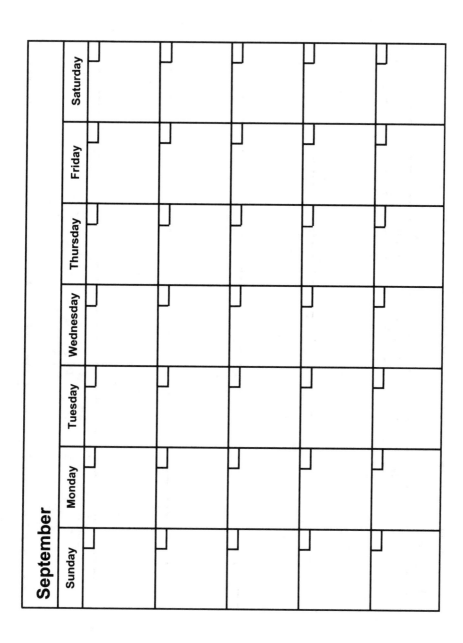

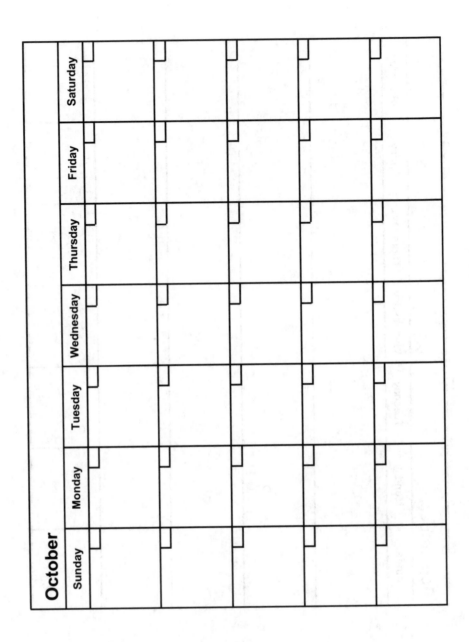

October

Sunday	Monday	Tuesday	Wednesday	Thursday	Friday	Saturday

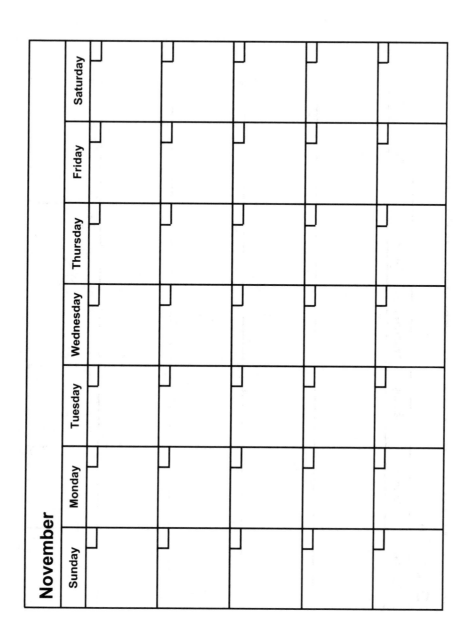

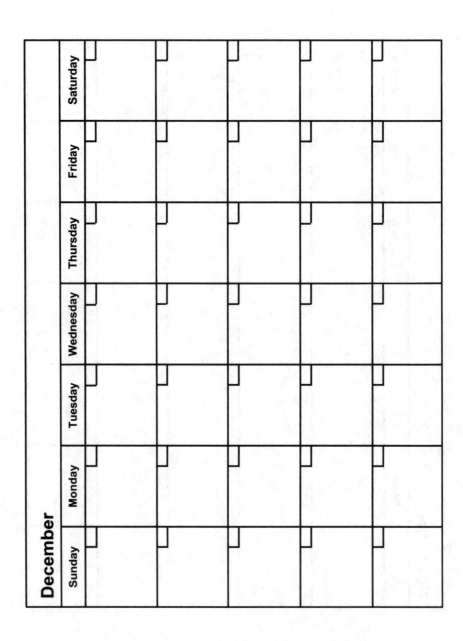

Resources of Sample Multiple-Choice Questions with Explanatory Answers

Appendix C contains a list of resources you can use to sharpen your skills in taking exams with multiple-choice questions.

Although the Strategies & Tactics books are intended for use in studying for the Bar Exam, many students use them to study for first-year courses. Each book contains hundreds of practice questions, and each question has a fully explained answer that analyzes, in detail, every answer option.

Strategies & Tactics for the MBE, Sixth Edition
by Steven L. Emanuel
ISBN 9781454873129

Strategies & Tactics for the MBE 2, 2nd Edition
by Steven L. Emanuel
ISBN 9781454833031

Strategies & Tactics for the FINZ Multistate Method, Fourth Edition
by Steven Finz and Alex Ruskell
ISBN 9781454873143

The Glannon Guides are topic-specific books that intersperse sophisticated multiple-choice questions—neither too difficult nor unrealistically straightforward—throughout the text. Correct and incorrect answers are explained, and the authors offer valuable techniques for test taking.

Glannon Guide to Bankruptcy, Fourth Edition
by Nathalie Martin
ISBN 978-1-4548-4689-5

**Glannon Guide to Commercial Paper and Payment Systems,
Third Edition**
by Stephen M. McJohn
ISBN 978-1-4548-4690-1

**Glannon Guide to Constitutional Law: Individual Rights and Liberties,
Second Edition**
by Brannon Padgett Denning
ISBN 978-1-7355-4687-1

Glannon Guide to Contracts, Second Edition
by Theodore Silver and Stephen Hochberg
ISBN 978-1-4548-5017-5

Glannon Guide to Criminal Law, Fourth Edition
by Laurie L. Levenson
978-1-4548-5013-7

Glannon Guide to Criminal Procedure, Third Edition
by John Kip Cornwell
ISBN 978-1-4548-5009-0

Glannon Guide to Evidence
by Michael Avery
ISBN 978-1-4548-5003-8

Glannon Guide to Professional Responsibility
by Dru Stevenson
ISBN 978-1-4548-6215-4

Glannon Guide to Property, Third Edition
by James Charles Smith
ISBN 978-1-4548-4691-8

Glannon Guide to Sales, Second Edition
by Scott J. Burnham
ISBN 978-0-7355-0966-5

Glannon Guide to Secured Transactions, Second Edition
by Scott L. Burnham
ISBN 978-1-4548-3006-1

Glannon Guide to Torts, Third Edition
by Richard L. Hasen
ISBN 978-1-4548-4688-8